MASTERING THE CEO'S GREATEST CHALLENGE

MASTERING THE CEO'S GREATEST CHALLENGE

Strategies for Staying Cool in the Executive Hot Seat

MICHAEL H. KAHN, PHD

MASTERING THE CEO'S GREATEST CHALLENGE
Strategies For Staying Cool In The Executive Hot Seat

iUniverse books may be ordered through booksellers or by contacting:

iUniverse LLC
1663 Liberty Drive
Bloomington, IN 47403
www.iuniverse.com
1-800-Authors (1-800-288-4677)

Because of the dynamic nature of the Internet, any web addresses or links contained in this book may have changed since publication and may no longer be valid. The views expressed in this work are solely those of the author and do not necessarily reflect the views of the publisher, and the publisher hereby disclaims any responsibility for them.

Any people depicted in stock imagery provided by Thinkstock are models, and such images are being used for illustrative purposes only. Certain stock imagery © Thinkstock.

ISBN: 978-1-4917-3871-9 (sc)
ISBN: 978-1-4917-3870-2 (hc)
ISBN: 978-1-4917-3869-6 (e)

Library of Congress Control Number: 2014911547

Printed in the United States of America.

iUniverse rev. date: 09/19/2014

The poem "Pausing" is from the book Juicing by Paul Reps.
It is used with permission by Paul Rep's niece, Roslyn R. Nelson, 2012.

The cartoon in chapter 4 was created and copyrighted by Jules Feiffer in 1974.
It is used with permission by Jules Feiffer 2012.

This is a wonderful book, and is certainly worth reading. The approach Michael Kahn has taken is very consistent with my own hardiness approach. In particular, these two approaches show how the most productive approach to dealing with the stressful circumstances of life is to throw oneself into the courageous and difficult process of turning the stresses from potential disasters into growth opportunities instead. This fulfilling process takes courage and hard work. In his own life, Kahn's serious physical illness provided the recognition that lots needed to be done to turn what was happening into psychosocial advance. It is not surprising to me that he was provoked in this by an article by Suzanne Kobasa, who at the time was a graduate student member of my hardiness research team. The team was studying individual difference in how Illinois Bell Telephone employees responded to a dramatic disruption of the telephone industry. Soon after, Deborah M. Khoshaba and I developed a validated hardiness training program that took a similar direction to the approach outlined by Kahn in his book. In all this, Kahn's life process following his physical illness is a fine example of recognizing the difficulty and stressfulness of life, and the need to use one's resources to turn this to advantage.

Salvatore R. Maddi, PhD

Professor, Department of Psychology and Social Behavior, University of California, Irvine; winner of the 2012 American Psychological Foundation Gold Medal Award for Lifetime Contributions to Psychology in the Public Interest; coauthor, *Resilience at Work: How to Succeed No Matter What Life Throws at You*

For my loving family,

Joyce, Lisa, & Joshua

and

In memoriam,

Irving & Florence Kahn

Alvin R. Mahrer

"PAUSING"

—Rosebud Conversation from *Juicing* by Paul Reps

The longer the pause
the fewer the flaws

In the pause your nerve
network resting in
consummate ease

Imagine pause as a vitamin
as big as an elephant

"Why pause?"
Why go out of breath?

Breath paused
heart paused
heart paused
life paused
into the next moment life

We pause between words said
in slow step
seeing   hearing   replying
as bliss this

Need you run about
unguided?

If you don't guide you
who will?

If you guide you can you
compute the uncounted
strings tying your
exquisite package
together?

CONTENTS

SECTION I

THE PERSONAL SIDE OF SUCCESS

SECTION II

THE MYTH OF NATURAL TALENT

SECTION III

ESSENTIALS OF PEAK PERFORMANCE

SECTION IV

MANAGING THE WORK DAY

LIST OF ILLUSTRATIONS

PREFACE

Every book has a story. This one began with a pivotal life event that happened to me forty-one years ago. An acute disease suddenly attacked and damaged my kidneys. I have lived with stage three kidney disease and the threat of further deterioration ever since. As I reflect on how that event changed my life, I consider it one of the more beneficial things that ever happened to me! You see, if I had not gotten sick a couple of months before my thirtieth birthday, the impetus to master the methods described in this book and to live a more informed and fulfilling life would not have happened.

The medical crisis happened in 1974, two years prior to completing my doctorate degree. I was besieged by the converging distress of completing the research for my dissertation, starting my first professional job, dealing with marital strife that ended in divorce several years later, and raising a young child. The cause or prognosis of the kidney disease that hit could not be determined. I was terrified that my life might end early, or at least be severely compromised by kidney failure. Having delayed so many of life's gratifications in order to complete my doctoral degree, I was just on the threshold of engaging life fully.

The crisis was a powerful wakeup call. It resulted in my mission to learn how to manage my professional and personal ambitions while taking good care of my health, relationships, and the many matters that are part of sustaining a fulfilling life. Had it not happened, I most likely would have lived my life like the more typical ambitious person: pushing forward in high-achievement mode while vanquishing self-care to a much lower-level priority. The hidden costs of such a lifestyle would have surfaced at a later point in life when my work style and lifestyle were more deeply set, and when it might have been too late to repair losses.

It is in this very personal context that this book evolved out of a lifetime of searching for what it takes to function optimally when faced with ambition, a lot of responsibility, and the desire to have a healthy and fulfilling personal life. I share my personal story with you because it sets the background for my practical and committed approach to the coping strategies and principles outlined in this book. This is the book I wish I had access to "back when." I hope it will make it easier for you to acquire the mental, emotional, interpersonal, and practical skills you need to function optimally, to sustain good health, and to have a fulfilling career and life. That is your greatest challenge as a CEO.

Once I recovered from the shock of having my body break down, I became fiercely determined to make the most of my life. I had to make sense of what had happened and what I could do to prevent a recurrence.

My investigation led me to the field of psychoneuroimmunology—the study of the interaction between psychological processes and the nervous and immune systems of the human body. I then narrowed my focus to health psychology—the study of the relations among psychological factors, behavior, and physical health and illness. In essence, I arrived at a more comprehensive understanding of what had probably happened to me: my immune system was weakened by the chronic stress I had been enduring and it broke down, making me vulnerable to a pathogen that attacked my kidneys.

From that point on, my mission has been to identify the factors that can be controlled to enhance health, well-being, and optimal functioning. And there is a lot! For me, that framework gave me a path I could take to engage life fully and to flourish. It is notable that the widespread belief at the time of my illness—and regrettably still common—was that when stress is part of the problem, you need to reduce or eliminate those activities that are distressing. That option was not acceptable to me. I had a life to live and things to do. I was not willing to compromise my goals.

I knew growing my career and my business meant I would have to develop my capacity to manage bigger and more complex pressures. Therefore, there would be many times that would be stressful. I needed methods that would serve me for the rest of my life.

Perhaps it was a coincidence, perhaps not, when I then came upon the now classic study by Suzanne Kobasa, PhD.[1] As a member of the Illinois Bell Study conducted by Salvatore Maddi, PhD, her long-term research project was on the impact of stress on top AT&T executives when the company was breaking up in the 1970s. The executives were facing big stressors: they were either losing their jobs or being reassigned, often with relocation. Kobasa found that over a period of eight years, two different patterns emerged in the way these executives responded to the stress. People in one group became increasingly symptomatic.

They had more medical and psychological problems and symptoms, and more doctors' visits. They also had more marital and other interpersonal problems. In contrast, the second group showed no difference in symptoms during this stressful period as compared to before its onset. Surprisingly, they seemed healthier and more robust. They essentially rose to meet the challenge.

Drs. Kobasa and Maddi[2] referred to this second group as having a *stress-hardy personality*, characterized by:

- **Commitment**—having a sense of meaning and purpose that energizes and guided their lives
- **Challenge**—dealing with the inevitable changes and frustrations of life as challenges and opportunities for personal growth
- **Control**—taking ownership for those parts of their challenge where they could make improvements and letting go of those over which they had no control

I realized I could use this hardiness mind-set to regain a sense of control over my life, and I set about learning as much as I could about the best ways to manage stress. I have never stopped learning and improving. My personal mission, to learn the best ways to manage the pressures of life, became my professional one: to teach and train others. I often tell my clients that all the methods I train people to use have been personally field-tested by me.

The concept of the hardy personality serves as the touchstone for the strategies in this book. Dealing with ongoing distress is more than a phase. It is inherent in the life that I had chosen as an entrepreneur and that you have chosen as a rising player in the business world. If you embrace the mind-set of viewing pressures (stress) as *challenges*, you will persist in seeking better ways to deal with them.

In the CEO Stress Project,[3] a study I completed between 2004 and 2007, I brought to sixty-two CEOs and other high-level executives my interest and questions about the challenges high-level executives face. This book combines the findings from the interviews with other important resources ranging from expert research to philosophers to poets. It incorporates the key components of my Stress Management and Health Skills Enhancement Program,[4] as well as what I have learned during my years as a psychologist, coach, and businessman.

I hope this book will serve as your personal training manual while you are developing your capacity to take on any business role that is epitomized by the position of CEO, including high-level business or organizational executive positions and entrepreneurs. It contains practical solutions and personal insights that you can turn to when you feel frustrated and methods to guide you on the path toward mastering the personal interface between yourself and the challenges of your career. Let it be a source of inspiration to perform better and experience less distress and more fulfillment at work and in your personal life.

In Stephen Covey's words, here you will find an effective compass to guide your efforts. You also need, of course, a robust body, a vibrant spirit, and support from others to navigate the ever-changing circumstances of your life.

ACKNOWLEDGMENTS

The story of this book includes the people who have been instrumental along the way. My parents, Irving and Florence Kahn, instilled in me the mission to seek better ways to manage life's challenges, as well as the love and belief that I have what it takes to pull it off.

I was very fortunate to have three remarkable people shape my professional development. Alvin R. Mahrer, PhD, my first psychotherapist and professional mentor, guided me through a process of deep inner transformation to become my true self, and taught me how to be a humanistic psychotherapist and a disciplined writer. Marvin R. Skolnick, MD, and Donald P. Seelig, PhD, clinical mentors par excellence, provided models, support, and astute guidance in my quest to becoming a master psychotherapist.

I want to thank Jim Saflund, MBA, for suggesting I could do the CEO Stress Project; Ben Dean, PhD, for introducing me to coaching and providing a model for the interviews; Ruth Geesey for transcribing eight hundred pages of transcripts; Judy Feld, MCC, my coach, for helping me continually improve my ways of working; Margaret Foster, Linda Page, Lisa Kahn Schnell, and Marc Schulhof for invaluable editorial input during the early years of writing a newsletter; the mystery editor at iU for wading through the first complete version and for his very constructive feedback; Monica, the iU editor, for the final editorial refinements; Joe Kita, my editor-cum-pizzazz; and Jeff Csatari, for initial and concluding encouragement and editorial input.

To the executives who shared their personal perspectives in the interviews for the CEO Stress Project,[5] I thank you for making the time to pause and reflect on what has allowed you to thrive as you have pursued your career and personal goals. Many readers will benefit from your stories, as has my understanding of what it really takes to manage the CEO's greatest challenge well.

I am grateful to Stephen Covey, PhD, Richard R. Kilburg, PhD, Jim Loehr, EdD, Salvatore R. Maddi, PhD, Mort Orman, MD, Ernest Rossi, PhD, and Robert M. Sapolsky, PhD, for their contributions to my comprehension of key issues.

It was deeply comforting to have the continuing support of my children Lisa Kahn Schnell and Joshua S. Kahn. They helped me sustain my efforts through the many phases by their patience, respect, loyalty, and love.

The depth and power of my appreciation for Joyce Cooper-Kahn, PhD, is immeasurable. For the past thirty-five years, she has been, and thankfully still is, my wife, best friend, and buddy, as well as my business partner and most trusted editor.

Thank you all.

INTRODUCTION

Your greatest challenge as a CEO[6] is to manage your personal side as well as you manage your work demands. Predisposed to being absorbed by work pressures, you are likely to neglect other aspects of yourself and your life.

The same quality that makes for successful CEOs—the ability to meet business challenges with effective action—also makes it more likely you will be less attentive to your requirements as a feeling, thinking human being. To complicate the challenge, it is also likely you believe you should be able to meet your biological, psychological, social, and spiritual needs without the benefit of training, and you expect yourself to perform optimally 24/7.

As a psychologist, I say that is preposterous! Yet many people attempt to do just that in their quest to rise through the executive ranks of companies, or to develop a business as an entrepreneur. Some people actually pull it off rather well. However, more often people accept as givens the problems that arise from how they cope with the pressures as their careers evolve. Too often, achievement-oriented business people tolerate unnecessary and excessive distress, discouragement, strained personal relationships, increased risk of illness, and even poor work performance. Despite people genuinely doing their best and concern over the downside of their work efforts, they do not know a better way.

In this book, you will find information that I hope will someday be the focus of a required course on the basics of self-management[7] in the real world of business. Its focus is on the skills needed to manage yourself as you face the evolving challenges of your career, so you can function as Ming-Jer Chen, MBA, PhD, of the Darden School of Business, describes, as follows:

> Each of us possesses an inner force that enables us to be optimally effective in all aspects of life. This is the power of "one." Although a precise definition is elusive, in its purest conception the power of one is the essence—the values, competencies, even relationships—at our center. It is much

xxiii

more than an abstraction. Indeed, it has practical applications for day-to-day life that are pervasive and powerful.[8]

Consider this book your training manual to guide you toward developing and mastering the personal coping skills it actually takes to stay cool in the executive "hot seat." As you expand your mastery of these skills, you will increase your capacity to manage the growing pressures in your career and personal life. You will find that you can do more *without* a proportional increase in distress. You will be able to perform better because you will bring your best mental, physical, and emotional energy to each facet of your career and life. The result is what I call Synergy for Success.

The methods are designed to be simple and accessible. In this book you will find guidelines for honing the personal coping skills needed to regulate your mind, emotions, and body in order to keep yourself centered and composed. Then you can devote your best personal and professional resources to the demands you face. The gains in your satisfaction in the workplace and in your personal life work together in a synergistic way, one enhancing the other.

The book synthesizes guidelines from coaching, psychotherapy, and hypnosis that have been adapted for busy executives. However, to get the most from them, you must understand that it is human nature to return to the familiar under distressing circumstances. So you do need to train yourself by practicing the new skills often enough to integrate them into your lifestyle as habits and routines, making them the new normal that you will turn to automatically.

Foundations for Success

There are four overriding principles that form the foundation for the specific strategies that you will learn in this book.

Hardiness for Hard Times Mind-set

The Hardiness for Hard Times mind-set guides you to manage pressures in a take-charge way so each one becomes a *challenge* to find the best ways to deal with and learn from it. When you shift to a take-charge approach, you dissipate the distress that so often arises in the face of pressure. The Hardiness for Hard Times approach is an application of the research by Kobasa[9] and Maddi[10] on the hardy personality. It is characterized by commitment, challenge, and control. I have drawn on the work of Lerner and colleagues[11] as well, who demonstrated that executives with an enhanced sense of control show less anxiety and fewer physiological measures of stress than those who do not.

Focus on Self-Regulation of Your Mind-Body Operating System

The emphasis throughout the book is on learning to regulate your mind-body[12] system—your primary "operating system"—so you can sustain the optimal performance levels needed to deal with the pressures of your career and life.

Skill-Building Approach to Self-Improvement

The best way to sustain the process of self-improvement is by adopting a growth mindset.[13] Within that frame of mind, your prevailing focus is on building skills through deliberate practice. Your attention to building the skills required for personal fulfillment can live quite comfortably side by side with your efforts to achieve in the business world.

Personal Wisdom

It is by understanding your own characteristic nature—your operating patterns—that you will gain the personal wisdom needed to develop Synergy for Success. You will need to have a firm grasp on your typical reactions from the point of encountering a challenge to its resolution. What happens to you mentally and emotionally? What helps you to expedite that process? With this knowledge, you can *work the process*—you can take full ownership for seeking the best ways to deal with yourself so you can efficiently navigate through the obstacles that have been sticking points in the past.

Overview of the Book

The five sections of *Mastering the CEO's Greatest Challenge* build upon one another.

The first section provides an overview of what it takes to function well as a CEO, including the specific core ingredients you need to function optimally.

In the second section, you will find guidelines for what it takes to make self-improvements.

Specific strategies needed to perform well are presented in the third section.

The personal side of managing the workday is addressed in the fourth section.

The final chapter reviews the key elements that foster continuing success.

At the end of each chapter, guidelines in a section called Make It Happen help you formulate your plan of action—the actual steps you will take to foster mastery of the methods.

You may find that the best way to use the book is to skim it through to get a basic understanding of the framework. Then go back through and read the first four chapters to lay the groundwork for what follows. Next, select those aspects of your life that you are ready to address, and go directly to those chapters. Consider this your personal handbook for learning new skills, and come back to it as a resource for reinforcing those you have already mastered.

I wish you the best of whatever you need along the way toward mastering your greatest challenge.

Section I

THE PERSONAL SIDE OF SUCCESS

Introduction

Many CEOs epitomize one of the highest levels of human functioning. My fascination with these CEOs is that in order to deal well with so many business pressures, CEOs must have highly effective strategies, abundant personal resources, and supportive relationships. As such, they are inspiring and can serve as models for anyone who aspires to become a high-level business executive.

However, while there are established paths to acquire the knowledge and skills to be a business executive, often including formal business and leadership training, there are few systematic ways to prepare for managing the personal pressures inherent in the job.

In general, the challenges of a CEO are presumed to be an enormous undertaking. And for the most part,

> · · ·
> I just wish that in schools we were taught some of these basic things. We teach kids to be stressed.
> —Clinton Wingrove
> Project Participant
> · · ·

they are. To perform well as a CEO, it is not sufficient to be smart, knowledgeable, and shrewd. Nor is it enough to be educated in matters of business leadership and management. You also must know what it really takes, as a person, to reliably perform well. You must understand the essential mental, physical, emotional, and interpersonal elements from which optimal outward behavior emerges.

You need to be "in the know" about what a person needs, in practical and human ways, to pull it off. "How do I manage myself so I can function at my best when executing the duties of my role? What are the best ways to manage my personal and relationship needs, my emotional reactions, moods, and attitudes, so they don't interfere with my intended career objectives? How can I perform at my best in my career AND have a healthy and fulfilling life? How do exemplary CEOs manage these personal challenges? What does research tell us about how to perform optimally?"

As philosopher Alan Watts[14] noted, it sometimes seems almost as if there is a taboo about conveying the inside information—or perhaps those who we'd hope know don't know. The availability of insights and guidance on these matters is limited because access to CEOs and to their private side is limited for strategic reasons. Most successful business executives keep the personal side of the daily challenges they grapple with hidden from public view. They have an investment in maintaining a public persona in order to command the trust and respect they need to do their jobs. As one CEO I interviewed put it, "I think a lot of CEOs are absolutely afraid of being found out; that they're not real, that they really didn't generate all of the profits that they did last year, that they don't have control of everything in their lives."

After all, it is prudent for CEOs to appear in charge and optimistic about their employees and the public. Even the memoirs of highly regarded CEOs tend to minimize the personal side of their success. Yet their ability to effectively manage the human elements has a big impact on their capacity to achieve their goals.

"Finding them out" was the mission of my CEO Stress Project—not to prove they are human but to show others how their humanity comes into play as they face their challenges. I wanted to show how those who do well are good at mobilizing their resources to navigate the pressures and to produce good outcomes. In that way, this book is like a "manual of initiation"[15] a mentor might slip his or her protégé while embarking on a journey to become a successful high-level executive. The interviews were framed to gain information that would be useful in this regard.

Chapter 1 will provide you with a framework for understanding the main components needed to function optimally as a CEO. It starts with a clear guide to the CEO's challenges from a psychological perspective and then presents the rationale for the methods presented throughout the book. Chapter 2 provides an overview of what success means from a variety of different perspectives and then engages you in the process of identifying what success means for you.

Chapter 1

THE BATTLE WITHIN

To set out boldly in our work is to make a pilgrimage of our labors,
to understand that the consummation of work lies not only in what we have done,
but who we have become while accomplishing the task.

—David Whyte, *Crossing the Unknown Sea*

Your success as a CEO depends on your ability to make good assessments of situations, develop sound plans and strategies, move decisively to actions having positive outcomes, effectively deal with people—and do so over extended periods of time. You must focus on what is crucial while faced with the flow of huge amounts of information and multiple often-competing business, interpersonal, and personal pressures.

To consistently pull this off, you must excel at being able to have your wits about you so you can be focused, in command, and able to make wise decisions at any moment. Psychologists call this being in your *ideal executive performance state.*[16] You may find it more useful to think of it as being able to *stay cool in the executive hot seat.* In order for you to do that quickly and reliably, you need to master the most important and greatest challenge you face every day: managing your *mind-body operating system*—with its biological, psychological, social, and spiritual needs.

Work, like marriage, is a place you can lose yourself more easily perhaps than finding yourself. It is a place full of powerful undercurrents, a place to find ourselves, but also, a place to drown, losing all sense of our own voice, our own contribution and conversation.

—David Whyte

The importance of your mind-body operating system is obvious. As the source of all functional capacities, the mind-body needs to be performing optimally to produce the best output. What makes this the greatest challenge? The short answer is that there is an inherent conflict that exists for most CEOs: on one side is their inclination to be focused on the demands of leadership and the pressure to take action, while on the other side, there is the need to monitor

3

and manage their fundamental human needs in order to function at their best.

The struggle that ensues is dramatically captured in the movie *The Defiant Ones*, starring Sidney Poitier and Tony Curtis as two escaped convicts who are shackled together. Both want to be free, but each wants to dominate the other. So their arguments with one another undermine their forward progress. Eventually they come to the realization that in order for them to succeed in their primary goal, they must find ways to cooperate. Once the chains are removed, their efforts to dominate have been transformed into partnership and respect.

In the business world, we often think of this struggle in the context of a supervisor and a staff member, where there may be tension between the work expectations of the former and the personal needs of the latter. However, when you are the CEO, the struggle takes place within yourself. In your "inner drama," the supervisor side of you is putting pressure on the worker side to work faster-harder-longer-better to meet various company goals. The worker side may need:

- more time for all the work that goes into leading well (to get additional information, to thoughtfully consider options, to manage the various competing demands),
- time to rest when you are mentally or physically weary,
- a reduction in hours to deal with a pressing family matter.

The tension between these two facets of yourself[17] will never completely go away. Left unmanaged, this is by far the greatest source of distress there is. Yet by coming to terms with that reality and accepting ownership for managing it, you can direct your efforts toward mastery. Then you can expect to perform optimally and do what it actually takes to have a good life.

Here is how David Whyte,[18] whose insightful writings about the challenges of integrating one's soul into the workplace and managing the interface between self, work, and relationships,[19] eloquently captures the challenge.

Work is a constant conversation. It is the back and forth between what I think is me and what I think is not me; it is the edge between what the world needs of me and what I need of the world. Like the person to whom I am committed in a relationship, it is constantly changing and surprising me by its demands and needs but also where it leads me, how much it teaches me, and especially, by how much tact, patience and maturity it demands of me.

To help your conversations go better, you need a working understanding of the two sides. We start with a synopsis of what it means to function well as a CEO (your output) and what it takes to function optimally (your input). As the book evolves, you will learn specific skills that are keys to your mastery of the challenge.

Becoming a Wise Leader

The CEO's Performance

The frame of reference for the guidelines I provide is based upon a vision of the CEO as a *wise leader*[20]—"doing the right thing, in the right way, and against the right time frame." To accomplish that, the CEO's overriding task is to determine "what is happening to and in the organization, apply appropriate perspective and planning to decide what to do, and then to act in an appropriate and determined way."[21]

The CEO's Mind

Not surprisingly, the basic brain functions that enable the CEO to achieve these outcomes are called the *executive functions* of the mind (see figure 1.1). They are neurologically based mental skills that enable you to *supervise* yourself and to *coordinate and direct* your efforts to achieve a goal.[22]

The CEO's Brain: Seven Skills You Must Have

Restraint—able to stop and think about your own behavior and emotions

Flexibility—able to change course freely

Emotional Control—able to stay objective

Initiation—able to generate ideas, responses, and strategies

Scratch Pad Memory—able to remember details to complete a task

Planning/Organization—able to manage workflow

Quality Control—able to make sure the work is up to standard

Adapted from Cooper-Kahn and Dietzel 2008

Figure 1.1

Six Essential Resources for the Executive

With these executive brain functions in place, you have the basic tools needed to be fully functional. In order to optimize the use of those capacities, you must have the resources summarized below. You also need reliable methods to monitor and manage these essential resources, the subject of later chapters.

> ➤ **Efficient Operating System.** You must keep your basic machinery functioning well, and this requires you to have reliable and efficient strategies to regulate and replenish your energy stores. Despite being under continual pressure to expend energy, you can only function at your best if you are attentive to the core biopsychological necessities of your mind-body operating system. To maintain your operating system, you need to effectively set limits on the demands made of you and have good ways to restore your energy.

> ➤ **Executive Cool.** You must maintain your composure in the face of the often overwhelming pressures you face as CEO. You must be able to gather information and deliberate on the best course of action, even in the face of pressing demands. This requires being able to stay aligned with your role functions, contain your emotions, and make a quick recovery when you lose your cool.

6

> ➤ **Mental Prowess.** You must work effectively, be creative, and use good judgment when making decisions. This requires the ability to disengage from the pressures to get perspective, including input from others, and necessitates having systems in place that allow you to keep your brain and body fully charged.

> ➤ **Supportive Relationships.** You must create an optimal work environment with others in order to achieve your goals and maintain a sense of well-being. To do so, you must master interpersonal and communication skills, know how to develop key supportive relationships, and have strategies for getting the most from your relationships while setting appropriate limits on interpersonal demands.

> ➤ **Workflow Management Skills.** You must engage your daily work pressures in a manner that enables focus on those leadership functions that only you can do. This requires a mindset and a set of skills that guide you in your efforts to prioritize tasks and plan for who will accomplish them and when.

> ➤ **Sustainable Practices.** You must be able to manage your resources with a focus on functioning consistently well over time. To do so, you must have the self-wisdom to know your own needs and you must reliably use the self-care practices that meet them. It also necessitates that you conduct yourself in a manner that is congruent with your most important values.

Malfunction Junction

Most executives proclaim that they value taking good care of themselves and their resources, yet many tend to lose sight of this perspective. There are many reasons that this can happen.

Blinded by Ambition. Think about the traits that define most CEOs. They generally share a deep belief in their capacity to get results, a strong capacity to focus, and the determination to do whatever it takes to achieve their objectives.

Often referred to as having a type-A personality, most people who become CEOs are so driven to achieve their business goals that they neglect the cost of their highly driven behavior. The light shines so brightly on the road to business success that they neglect to take the car off the road long enough for refueling and basic maintenance. At some point, the neglect catches up with them and they end up at malfunction junction, surprised their vehicle has broken down.

This all makes sense when you understand the experience of such people. For most CEOs, work is a career, not a job. They get a deep sense of fulfillment from their careers. In fact, many find their job energizing and often prefer career-related matters to other activities in life, including rest. This makes them chronically vulnerable to depletion of their resources.

For many people striving to become a high-level executive, or for those new to the role, self-care and self-management are too often matters for which they do not have time. The experience of absorption into their work is deep, powerful, and compelling. With work as the center of their focus and the domain in which they spend the bulk of their time and energy, other aspects of life naturally get less attention. Often this is not so much a conscious decision but an omission that happens naturally and insidiously. They do not realize the needs they are neglecting are taking their toll. By the time the neglected areas reach their awareness, they are forced to deal with them because of a breakdown that causes an unplanned and significant interruption in work. This contributes to the misguided notion that managing one's needs and pressure are energy hogs!

Lack of Skills. There is a paradox that often exists for people who are good at managing business matters: they are good at taking charge of external problems but weak at managing their own needs. They are so results-oriented and focused on the bottom line that they do not want to be bothered by self-care. What they really want is a maintenance-free mind-body-spirit-relationship system that is reliable, efficient, and maintains a low profile.

Drawn to the Familiar. For many executives, the more they are drawn into the business world the further removed they become from nonwork aspects of life. They are prone to overvaluing the benefits of business, where they feel more competent and in control. Their greater sense of comfort, familiarity, and mastery within the business domain can set up an even stronger drift away from their other needs. Even when they sense something is troubling them, their tendency is to do what they do best, which is to focus even more on work. Downplaying the role of personal and social needs, they tend to override personal sources of frustration.

Poor Models. The challenge is further complicated by the fact that many CEOs lack good models for coping with pressures, either from the business world or in their personal lives. Even in the media, the images of public figures and successful high-level CEOs are often of those who are driven by ambition and the need for power, arrogance, and entitlement. The not-so-public costs of ambition-gone-awry show up behind closed doors. That is where the erosion of marriages, families, health, and life fulfillment happen—while the neighbors envy the appearance of success.

Hidden Costs

There is a price that must be paid somewhere for neglecting self-care.[23] People who are blinded by ambition unwittingly create the conditions where they are operating on an ever-increasing deficit of personal resources. As their energy becomes depleted, the executive functions of the mind are compromised.

Typically, this process and the price is hidden until it shows up as an erosion of an individual's usual mode of operation. As a person's resources run low, you may see deteriorating work performance, difficulty concentrating, poor decisions, and irritability. Work and personal relationships, as well as health, suffer. Determined to succeed, a person who is depleted is more vulnerable to quick fixes that are harmful in the long run, such as an overreliance on food, alcohol, medications, and other substances. The conditions gradually ripen for an intensified conflict between the work pressures and personal needs. As matters deteriorate, the individual unwittingly precipitates a serious mess up at work, or a personal health or relationship problem—the proverbial *wakeup call*—which then *must* be given attention. The worst-case scenario is burnout.

The tendency to need the wakeup call is an interesting side of human nature. It is especially notable when you contrast it with how much more mindful people often are of the maintenance requirements of their automobiles, which have replaceable parts. Expensive? Yes, but replaceable nonetheless. The machinery of our mind-body-spirit system, though somewhat resilient, does not have replaceable parts. The cost of breakdowns? Often immeasurable! And what of the erosion of primary personal relationships with life partners and children? The antidote? Make self-management high-level priorities.

Prioritizing Self-Management

Neither business experience nor traditional business education offer the training you need to master the art of managing yourself. This book is designed to help you learn to manage and care for yourself so you can operate from a position of inner composure, strength, competence, and health. Stephen Covey put it well[24]: "This is the single most powerful investment we can ever make in life—investment in ourselves, in the one instrument we have with which to deal with life and to contribute. We are the instruments of our own performance, and to be effective, we need to recognize the importance of taking the time regularly to sharpen the saw."

Valuing Your Most Vital Employe

Successful CEOs are deeply invested in performing at their best each day and over the long haul. They know they must be able to sustain optimal functioning over the ever-changing landscape of their careers and life. They do not tolerate functioning poorly and certainly have little patience for repeatedly making the same mistakes or for putting up with things that distract their attention or drain their good energy. Consequently, they actively seek better ways to take care of their basic needs and to manage the pressures of their work and personal life.

> *Success in the knowledge economy comes to those who know themselves——their strengths, their values, and how they best perform.*
>
> —Peter F. Drucker

The smart way for you to develop your career is to make self-management a high priority early in your career so it becomes a natural and routine part of your lifestyle. Once it becomes your new default mode, you will automatically apply the skills presented in this book at times of increased pressure. In this way, you both buffer yourself from the downward spiral often associated with stress and increase your capacity to handle it better.

Mastering Your Greatest Challenge

Your greatest challenge, is, like Max in *Where the Wild Things Are*,[25] to become the master of your inner wild parts—you must learn to tame the part of you that threatens to go after work goals with such abandon that you neglect the signs that your personal resources are running low. Mastering the challenge offsets the risk that a neglected need will become dominate over your ambition, such as a medical or relationship crisis. It also improves your work performance by the augmented energy from the synergy amongst the key aspects of work, self, and relationships.

For you to take on and sustain the challenge, you must be convinced that your current level of performance and satisfaction are at risk of suffering due to inadequate resources; you can integrate the methods in this book into your lifestyle so they become a natural part of how you conduct yourself; and the resulting synergy will prove to be a high return on your investment. You will need to read on and apply the methods to accomplish that.

The most important skill anyone can have is the relationship you have with yourself and how you come to love and appreciate yourself. Ultimately, there is only you.

—Pat Lynch
Project Participant

Should you expect the inherent inner battles to be eliminated? Of course not. Nevertheless, you can expect to have more respect for what it takes to keep the struggles in line and to have effective strategies to achieve that, thereby spending less time entangled in them. Then you can move more smoothly, quickly, and decisively into actions that are in your overall best interest.

My interviews showed that there are real people who are finding ways to not only minimize the typical pitfalls of the career success track but are living lives enriched by the integration of their careers with their relationships, and their personal interests, values, and needs. Most often we are not privy to their stories. These ambitious, highly respected, and successful business people are proud of the fact that they remain true to themselves. Their self-wisdom is evident in the way they manage themselves on a daily basis.

As one executive stated, "It is having a deep inner knowledge that allows you to live and love your life. That way, the things I'm doing in my work right now, and how I hold my work, are just the way I do it, not necessarily the way you do it, and it's perfect for me."

Alan Leis EdD, superintendent of schools in Naperville, Illinois, who has extensive training in leadership noted that a strong sense of identity is essential in order to be "an authentic person, and still step into the leadership role—and not lose yourself in the process."

Guiding Principles

The Hardiness for Hard Times approach to self-management focuses your efforts on strategies that give you the biggest return on your efforts.

> ➢ You take ownership for the necessity to manage yourself and make a *commitment* to doing so.
> ➢ You take *control* of the elements (the subject of the book) that leverage your efforts.
> ➢ You maintain a growth mind-set where self-management becomes a positive *challenge.*

The Synergy for Success model emphasizes the potentiating effects of managing work and personal life well. The model builds on important principles drawn from innovators in the fields of both psychology and business, including Stephen Covey,[26] W. Timothy Gallwey,[27] Richard Kilburg,[28] James Loehr,[29] Salvatore Maddi,[30] Ernest Rossi,[31] and Al Siebert,[32]

Figure 1.2 summarizes the model as the CEO's *personal success equation.*

	Role well-being
	Personal well-being
	Self-management
	Support system
+	Synergy amongst facets of life
$\sum$ =	Successful Performance & Fulfillment

Figure 1.2

Because your personal resources are the wellspring of both performance and fulfillment, *the necessity for maintaining highly effective self-management practices increases* as *the pressures of work and personal life increase.*

~.~

Make It Happen

I hope you will use this book as a guide in your quest to master the CEO's greatest challenge. To make that happen, it is essential you combine the information you gain with *action*. Start with small steps, and soon you will find that you have made real and significant changes. (In chapter 3 you will learn more about the process of making changes.)

Here are three steps you can take *now* to launch the process of mastering the challenge.

Step One. Create a document to keep track of the actions you initiate as you work through the book.

Step Two. Take a few minutes now to identify the three points in this chapter that resonate the most with you. Write a sentence or phrase about each.

Step Three. Which aspects of the challenge of being a CEO capture the essence of your strong and weak points? Write a sentence or phrase for each.

Chapter 2

SETTING YOUR SAILS FOR SUCCESS

One ship sails east,
And another west,
By the self-same winds that blow.
'Tis the set of the sails
And not the gales,
That tells the way we go.

—Ella Wheeler Wilcox, *'Tis the Set of the Sail—or—One Ship Sails East*

Of course, you want to be successful! However, that is not as straightforward a goal as it might seem. How well do you know what you mean by success? As performance experts often highlight, you must be very specific about what you are trying to accomplish in order to set the process of achieving it in motion.

I don't think the smartest people always succeed. They have the possibility of succeeding, but it's just some combination of personal and personal management skills that makes people succeed

—Project Participant

In his classic book *Think and Grow Rich*, Napoleon Hill[33] underscores the direct and indirect ways that being clear about our goals influences our path to success. Similarly, Stephen Covey[34] reminds us to be careful about the ladder we climb to success—we want to be sure it is up against the right wall. After all, when we have in our sights the goals we most want to achieve, we are at our most engaged.

Here's how one CEO described the importance of working in concert with his goals: "When you do something you are emotionally committed to and you believe is important, it mitigates any type of job stress you might have. Then, all the usual distressing things are just part of doing a job."

Nevertheless, your career, the people you deal with at work and in your personal life, and your own personal needs will regularly challenge what matters the most to you as surely as a child tests the values of his or her parents. You can maintain your equanimity by reminding yourself that, just as your child is not being "bad" when testing you, neither are the people or activities in your life that compete for your attention inherently unreasonable. Each is simply trying to get what it wants and needs—energy, attention, time, emotional involvement, and/or money. When you feel distress at those times, it means you have work to do. You must clarify your priorities and decide what is best for you to do. You must grapple with questions like, "Is this something I want or need to do?" "Is this worth the resources I would need to commit?" "Is this the right time for me to do this?" "How will this affect my company or my family?"

Of course you cannot always prevent the collision of two very important matters. One of the more acutely distressing times for me is when I am at work trying to resolve an urgent matter and my commitment to be with my family requires that I leave the matter behind to be with them.

You can prepare yourself to manage many of those challenges by using the information and exercises presented in this chapter to learn:

- how to determine the types of success you want (yes, there is more than one),
- how to crystallize your vision of the good life,
- how a personal positioning system (PPS) can help you navigate toward your goals.

Key Dimensions of Success

How will you know success when you see it? What will it look like across various timelines: in the moment-to-moment experiences of the day, at the end of the day, week, and over the course of your life? Whatever the specifics of your goals, this book will help you achieve success in the following three key dimensions.

Success as Performance

When you see success through the lens of performance, you focus on what it takes to get results. Success as performance means you are able to reliably and consistently apply the full force of your capacity to your endeavors and make them turn out the way you intend. It means maintaining your ideal performance state (IPS), a term coined by performance psychologist James E. Loehr.[35]

Performing successfully as a CEO generally means two main things: providing the leadership your company needs to thrive over the long term; reliably sustaining your ideal performance state over time.

Success as Fulfillment

Coaches, psychologists, business leaders, sages, and spiritual leaders use several different terms to refer to success: happiness, a good life, a meaningful life, and an authentically happy life. All these terms suggest a set of core ingredients for success as fulfillment. The two perspectives that best capture success as fulfillment are the psychological and the spiritual.

Psychological Fulfillment. When you participate in activities that engage you because they interest you and are enjoyable, separate from external pressures or rewards, the involvement is satisfying. Academic and research psychologist Martin Seligman[36] states, "Authentic happiness comes from identifying and cultivating your most fundamental strengths and using them every day in work, love, play, and parenting."

Spiritual Fulfillment. When your involvement is motivated by a sense of desire, meaning, and purpose that goes beyond your personal needs and is independent of material gains, it is satisfying. Philosopher, academic, and mystic Rabbi Marc Gafni offers, "Happiness is a natural result of the way your values help weave the singular tapestry of your life, lived in response to your call."[37]

Synergy for Success

While achievement in terms of career and wealth are often touted as the definition of success, these are not necessarily the stuff of happiness. The results of research by psychologists,[38] as well as the wisdom of philosophers and sages, suggest wealth and work achievements are not directly correlated with happiness. A deeper and more compelling sense of contentment derives from succeeding at your career endeavors *and* meeting your personal and social needs, thus creating synergy amongst the various facets of your life.

The strategy for sustaining success that I am unequivocally advocating is a *lifestyle* built on the synergy amongst these overlapping aspects of your life: work endeavors, personal relationships, and self as a separate person. It is this synergy that generates the energy and promotes the fulfillment across areas that creates sustainability.

Work-Life Balance? Not Really. I've never found the popular notion of "work-life balance" useful. It promotes juggling and multitasking as the primary methods of calibration, and this sets up a competitive dynamic between the two. The outcome is too often like a pendulum that swings in a large arc. It also smacks too much of the sort of thing "you know you ought to do." Instead, I use the Synergy for Success model to emphasize that the parts are aspects of a whole *system*. Then there is incentive to manage each dimension well and to pay attention to the interplay amongst them, since each one benefits from the others. This sets up a *teamwork* approach, a true interdependence where each part of you is invested in the other doing well. It is a genuinely powerful strategy—limited, in large part, by the extent in which you commit to it. You cannot fake it.

Adhering to the Synergy for Success model also provides mental guardrails to protect you from being blinded by ambition and the pressures of the moment. Even during those phases when you are enmeshed in achieving a work goal, the model makes it easier to remember and respect the vital role of attending to your personal matters in the service of performing well.

Many books about achieving business and career goals exist. However, often these only intensify the CEO's greatest challenge by focusing on outcomes while downplaying the personal side. The present strategy is to foster your best output by using strategies that effectively manage the personal side of your success equation. You, of course, may place a higher value on one dimension of success (career, family, personal) than on another. What matters is that you manage each aspect well enough that it is a reliable resource for you and not a drain on the energy needed when dealing with each of the others.

Appreciating the Good Life

How will you know success when you see it? What will it look like across various time lines: in the moment-to-moment experiences of the day, at the end of the day, week, and over the course of your life? Let's consider what it takes to build your own vision of the good life.

The Hazards of Speed

While we focus a great deal of effort these days on increasing the speed with which we can accomplish tasks, as a general approach the craving for speed runs counter to what it actually takes to develop and sustain most elements of a successful life. Still, when things go poorly, the tendency is to seek the quick fix. We are so eager to feel better and to make the situation better in a hurry that we may pass over substantive solutions, those that build a durable foundation. In our search for the quick and easy solution, real progress is retarded.

The most important thing is to get in touch with what makes you happy; what turns you on, what lights your fire. If you have no juice, you're going nowhere.

—Pat Lynch
Project Participant

Remember, one of the greatest risks is that in your zeal to sprint ahead in your work, you can get caught up in an ongoing but futile attempt to "win" the race without realizing what you are running past. This leads to erosion in other facets of your life. All too often people only arrive at this realization after wearing themselves down and/or doing permanent damage to their most important relationships. Sometimes it is only late in life that people come to the recognition of the damage they have done, and then it is even more devastating.

The adage that life is a marathon and not a sprint certainly needs to be a guiding perspective in your efforts to sustain success. Focus on maintaining a good steady performance while retaining sufficient energy in your reserves for the hills, wind, and occasional sprints.

Life as Journey

One way to offset the hazards of speed is to appreciate the process of life. I remember well a popular poster in the late 1960s that showed a child gazing at a path that unfolded in front of her without a clear end point. The caption read *Life is a journey, not a destination.*

Experiencing life as a journey leads to respect for the flow of life—how events that have happened contribute to the present and how the present is helping to shape the future. In this way, we are able to genuinely value the small, incremental steps that become bigger developments. Valuing these small steps toward the larger goal helps us to stay on the path even when the going gets difficult. But it also helps us to understand that we may end up getting to our goals via a different path than we had originally planned.

Don't be saying, when I get to the top of the mountain I'm going to be happy, because if you're not enjoying the process, it's not worth it. There is no amount of stress that's worth what's at the end of the line, so you really should try and enjoy that process.

—Jon Coile
Project Participant

For some, this kind of wisdom emerges out of life experience, such as Dawn Sweeney, president and CEO of AARP Services, who had the terrible misfortune of losing a daughter at age thirteen months: "That is a life-changing experience more than just about anything you can possibly imagine. From that came a big growth opportunity for me where I really got it that you don't have a lot of control over anything. The way I have approached my business life, since then especially, has been, you've got to have a vision, you've got to have a big direction you're going for, and then you've just got to be enormously flexible. And you can't get too invested in a path."

Living through major life events also puts the pressures of work life into perspective. People whose lives have been compromised by disabilities, illnesses, or grief over the loss of a loved one (or other circumstances) are forced to come to terms with what really matters. In so doing, the tendency to get worked up over small things tends to recede.

One executive who lost her teenage son in an automobile accident noted that before the tragedy she thought she always had good clarity on her priorities. "The difference is that I could sometimes be persuaded to take on too much, but now I am never persuaded. Because the ultimate worst consequence has happened to me, there is nothing anybody can do to me. That's why no matter how much you ask me, it doesn't matter. It's because I don't care what people think. I do have to be careful because it's not that I don't care about you as a person or anything, but I'm not a stake holder in what people think."

Tom Beerntsen, president and CEO of the Heritage YMCA Group, whose wife was severely attacked and almost killed, advised that you should "never lose track of the job you were hired to do, and realize it is not the reason you are alive. My job has been stressful, but my personal life has been more stressful and it makes you realize that there's big things and then there's big things. The job at the end of the day is what you do, and what you are is much more important."

Do you have to go through difficult times before you can fully appreciate life is a journey? I don't think so. You can borrow the life experience of others to adjust your own approach. No matter how you come by this more measured perspective, it shifts your experience. Take a moment now to imagine how much better your life could be if it was informed by your coming to terms with the natural limits of life without being led there by a crisis.[39]

To ensure you have the internal guidance system that will keep you aligned with your good life, you need to formulate a clear image of the life you want to lead. The following guidelines can help you engage your deeply held values. As you do these exercises, remember it is these deeply held values that will also ignite your power.

Reflecting on a Life Worth Living

As you look within to find what constitutes the good life for you, it is important to free yourself from the usual constraints of logic and criticism. That is harder than it might seem. Fortunately, techniques drawn from self-hypnosis offer a powerful and straightforward way to tap into your inner wisdom.

The Good-Life Self-Hypnosis Exercise. Find a comfortable spot where you can be free of distractions and protected from interruptions. Set a timer to go off in fifteen minutes. All clichés aside, tell yourself you are going into your imagination to a safe or happy place where you are free from the usual pressures. To foster the shift from the usual conscious way of being engaged and to trigger a sense of calmness, do the following: take a deep breath, hold it for a few seconds, and then let it out slowly while letting your eyes drift slowly closed. Focus on each breath as you would the gentle rocking of a rowboat on a pond.

As you begin to sense that you are drifting into a calmer state, picture yourself going in your imagination to your safe or happy place. It could be a real place, such as a favorite beach, or fully imaginary, like resting on a cloud. All that matters is that you immerse yourself in this special experience so you feel safe and free from all the usual pressures, including the use of logic. By using all your senses to experience this special place, your brain responds as if you are physically there. Your brain does not differentiate between reality and your good imagination. You will gradually drift into a comfort zone, and your mind and body will calm down. The experience is much like watching a sunset or a fire in a fireplace, or the feeling of drifting off to sleep or first awakening.

Once you are in your special place, imagine it is ten or twenty years from now or maybe that you have retired. Reflect back upon your life and see what it is that you are most proud of, what gave you the greatest fulfillment, and what your biggest regrets are.

The goal at this juncture is to identify the essential components of your personal success equation, the elements that reflect your essential nature.[40] What is it that will enable you to have peace of mind, to feel that you have lived a life worth living? You may find that doing this exercise several times increases your comfort with it, and you gain a little more understanding of your good life each time.

Composing Your Good-Life Narrative

Once you have a vision of your good life, it will help to create a written document. Some people do this by creating a list of the essential elements or composing a written narrative. Others prefer a visual representation to help them organize their ideas, often called a mind-map. Each component shown in the sample in figure 2.1 can be broken down into components including key values and specific activities.

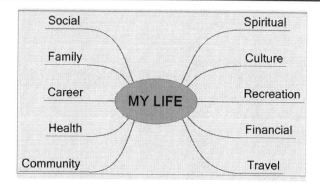

Figure 2.1

This will be a working document and the specifics may change over time as you work with it. However, the essential elements will endure and reflect your unique self, just like your fingerprint. Once you have captured the essence of what matters most to you, you will find that when push comes to shove, you are better prepared to defend the sanctity of your vision.

Identifying Your Core Personal Values

Remember, every pressure you encounter requires that you uphold your needs, values, and goals. You can prepare yourself to set the boundaries that accomplish that by using the rating scale shown below in figure 2.2.[41] It is an easy way to start formulating your profile. You will get the most power out of this exercise by completing the ratings and doing a short narrative for each of the core values.

As you consider your core values, it is important to approach them with sufficient depth to identify the following two crucial components.

What is it that makes this an *essential* part of your success equation? That is, how does it reflect who you are as a person? What about it is vital for you to function well? What are the absolutes that you must have for each? Formulate your preferred range of each and the limits beyond which you will not go. The aim is to set your parameters for what really works for you and what does not.

Core Personal Values	
Physical health	1 2 3 4 5
Sleep	1 2 3 4 5
Nutrition	1 2 3 4 5
Physical exercise	1 2 3 4 5
Relationships with family	1 2 3 4 5
Relationships with friends	1 2 3 4 5
Relationships with staff	1 2 3 4 5
Feeling proud of how I managed the day's pressures	1 2 3 4 5
Sense of accomplishment	1 2 3 4 5
Self-renewal	1 2 3 4 5
Recreation	1 2 3 4 5
Minimal daily distress	1 2 3 4 5
Peace of mind	1 2 3 4 5

Key 1 = Unessential **2** = Slightly important **3** = Important **4** = Very Important **5** = Essential

Figure 2.2

The challenge here is for you to get beyond the common feeling of "I know I should do this" and focus instead on what is important enough to you that you will choose to do it consistently. After all, it is your sense of conviction about your core values that dictates your choices about where you put your efforts. And while people often feel that they *have to* do something because of their obligation to the company or another cause, the truth is that we conduct our lives as though there are many more "have-tos" than is really the case.

The more you take full ownership for yourself and your life, the more you realize that you *do* have choices. You may not like the consequences of all of your choices. Nevertheless, it is essential that you step back from the "in-your-face" pressures to reaffirm your basic needs and values. This is the most powerful antidote to "stress" that there is, bar none!

. . .

Is this decision I am about to make going to further me towards my life mission, or does it take me away from it?

—Aadil Palkhivala
Project Participant

. . .

23

Modify your profile as needed, and be sure to reappraise it at regular intervals. If you need to boost your commitment and clarity, review your list of core values once each day for two weeks to get them embedded in your "operating system." Then, set aside fifteen minutes each week to return to the task of reviewing and adjusting your core values. Some people find that the use of longer sessions (such as thirty minutes once each month, or sixty minutes once each quarter) serve to deepen their commitment to core values. In these ways, you take charge of the challenges that you *will* encounter by reaffirming your boundaries.

While there are times when flexibility is warranted, you will need to learn how to uphold each core value in a way that maintains your integrity. For example, one CEO is devoted to being present with his children at certain times of the day, such as the hour before bedtime. He feels these times are essential to building the kind of relationship with them that is vital to his vision of the good life. Some CEOs have come to believe they require certain amounts of sleep, exercise, and nutrition each day, so they make sure these self-care practices happen.

Personal Asset Allocations

Physical Energy

1. I can count on having good physical energy throughout the workday. 1 2 3 4 5
2. I am pleased with my physical energy at work. 1 2 3 4 5

Mental Energy

3. My concentration is good throughout the day. 1 2 3 4 5
4. I consistently meet challenges with clear thinking. 1 2 3 4 5

Emotional Resilience

5. When I encounter frustration I can reliably recover my equilibrium in 1 2 3 4 5
   short order and deal with the challenge in a proactive manner.
6. I can count on my capacity to flexibly shift from disappointment to 1 2 3 4 5
   enthusiasm throughout the workday.

[continued]

Figure 2.3A

Status Check

Before learning more about how to stay on your path, it is a good idea to take stock of where you are starting from. How are you doing now at managing your core values? One way to assess this is to rate the core values in figure 2.2 a second time giving each a score for the extent to which you are doing well at upholding each (five is the highest rating). When you are ready for more input, you can also get your life partner and/or best friend to do a rating, and use the Personal Asset Allocations checklist in figure 2.3 to rate how your current methods are influencing your functioning.

Personal Asset Allocations

Creativity

7. My level of creativity is good throughout the day.   1 2 3 4 5
8. I am pleased with my capacity for creativity throughout the day.   1 2 3 4 5

Stress Management

9. When I leave the office, I feel satisfied with the quality of my productivity. 1 2 3 4 5
10. When I arrive at home at the end of the day, I feel good about how I
    managed the pressures of the day.   1 2 3 4 5

Work-Personal Life Synergy

11. My personal life provides a reliable foundation that enhances my work
    performance.   1 2 3 4 5
12. The satisfaction and sense of accomplishment I derive from my work
    contributes to my sense of well-being and ability to enjoy my
    personal life.   1 2 3 4 5
13. I am able to reaffirm my values and principles when faced with conflicts
    between work and personal life pressures.   1 2 3 4 5

Key 1 = Rarely True; 2 = Sometimes True; 3 = True; 4 = Frequently True;
5 = Always True

Figure 2.3b

Recognizing the Disparity

Take a look at the difference between your priorities and the way you are currently living your life. How is the discrepancy influencing your life now? What do your observations tell you about how involved you are in each area? What does this mean to you? How is this influencing your life now? How is it likely to affect the life you want to live over the longer term?

It is by monitoring the congruence of your behaviors with your core values that you set the foundation for gaining mastery over the CEO's greatest challenge.

Your awareness of the disparity between what you desire and the way things actually are is a crucial wellspring of motivation to make improvements. Use the guidelines in this book to take charge of bringing the two into better alignment.

Making Your Vision Real

The same self-hypnosis technique that you used to explore your core values can help you to make your vision of the good life a reality. This time while in your safe place, imagine you are writing your memoirs, or sharing your wisdom with a grandchild who just completed college and is starting out in life. As you imagine telling your story, be sure to identify the *specific* steps you took that contributed most to your success in creating your good life. Be certain also to point out the potential pitfalls you identified along the way. Write down what you discovered in as much detail as you can. You may be amazed at the wisdom you find within yourself and the practical knowledge that emerges. I have found people are generally quite realistic and creative when they use this method. It taps into the part of you that already "knows" what really works for you.

Using Your Personal Positioning System (PPS)

Human nature being what it is, no matter how self-directed and self-disciplined you are, you will find it helpful to have a systematic way to keep aligned with your personal operating system and its resources, and your life goals. Imagine what it would be like if you had the equivalent of a global positioning system (GPS) for your mind-body operating system and your agenda. It would enable you to monitor where you are each day in relation to your personal needs, values, goals, and demands. The idea for developing such a "device," a personal positioning system (PPS), came to me during a sailing vacation.

Today's world presents numerous challenges to maintaining one's focus. It offers a plentiful supply of interesting but unimportant stimulation, whereas many important stimuli lack interest. Thus, people must ignore much of what surrounds them.

—Kaplan and Berman 2010

Some years ago, while cruising the Caribbean islands on a sailboat, I had the opportunity to observe my friends and co-captains, James and Richard, as they navigated over the course of two weeks. Decisions needed to be made on an ongoing basis in order to plan, monitor, and adjust all aspects of our trip to ensure our safety and to maximize enjoyment. Would the weather allow us to sail smoothly through the open-water leg of our trip? If we spent an extra day on the open water, would we need more provisions before we started? What were the advantages and disadvantages of one route over another? How could they trim the rigging or adjust our course to get us efficiently to our destination? Were the course adjustments effective?

Along the way, James and Richard continuously discussed the pros and cons of various course corrections and adjustments to the rigging. Each decision incorporated a reading from the GPS to determine present location in relation to key preplanned set points on the way to our destination.

Watching this ongoing drama unfold, I was impressed by the crucial value of persistently monitoring all systems and making adjustments accordingly. Decisions were based on an assessment of the interplay between current location, weather and sea conditions, stock of provisions, the well-being of the crew, and short-and long-range goals. I realized I was observing the essential components for successful navigation that could be applied to any of life's journeys. This was the germinal seed for the PPS, which metaphorically captures a system of monitoring and regulating one's attention and actions based on key data points.

You may find the metaphor of sailors and the GPS, when applied to your ongoing life in the form of a personal positioning system (PPS), helps you visualize your daily life and the process of calibrating and recalibrating to stay on course.

Specific guidelines for developing and using a PPS are presented in chapter 4.

The Boundaries of Time

It is human nature, especially the younger you are, to live as if there are no limits. If you really want to bring power to your efforts to develop the good life, use your calendar well. How much time do you have for your goals, including the larger timeline of the stages of your life? Pay attention to the markers along the way, especially birthdays—they are the real signposts of your life. It is far better to reflect on where you are in the grand scheme of your life with each passing year than to push that aside, only to be clobbered at some later point in time when you are much farther down the road.

Make It Happen

The exercises in this chapter are designed to engage you in the process of setting your course based on your goals and values. Completing the exercises will establish the hook that makes the guidelines in the rest of the book really take hold.

Step One. Do the good-life self-hypnosis exercise (see p. 32) at least once for reflecting back on a life worth living. Take notes on what you discover.

Step Two. A log is a useful and simple way for keeping track of actions you have taken and monitoring progress. It will help you to hold yourself accountable so that your intentions become actions. Use the log you created in the exercise at the end of chapter 1 to record your actions toward identifying your core values and for brief comments and observations. Simply noting you did something you intended to do can offer a sense of accomplishment that will boost your energy and spirit.

Step Three. If you have not yet completed the other exercises in this chapter, decide now when you will. Make an entry in your calendar for when you will do each exercise and select a target date for when you intend to have completed all of them. How serious are you about mastering the CEO's greatest challenge? Completing the exercises will set you on the path.

Section II

THE MYTH OF NATURAL TALENT

Introduction

According to all known laws of aviation,
there is no way a bee should be able to fly.
Its wings are too small to get its fat little body off the ground.
The bee, of course, flies anyway
because bees don't care what humans think is impossible.

—Narrator, *Bee Movie*[42]

The power of our beliefs over our capacity to perform was dramatically demonstrated in 1954 by Roger Banister, who persisted in his efforts to run a mile in fewer than four minutes and succeeded. Prior to his achievement, many athletes had tried to break what was believed to be a physiological barrier of four minutes, beyond which humans could not go.[43] Subsequently, many people have accomplished the feat. Since it is unlikely human physiology has changed that much, it is now believed that what made the difference was his belief he could make it happen.

Some people take this phenomenon to the extreme and say, "You can do anything you set your mind to." While that is not necessarily true, many of the limitations people accept are also not true. It is a basic tenet of this book that with specific goals to motivate you and solid strategies to guide you, you can expand your capabilities.

In order for you to succeed at making the self-improvements presented in this book, you need to know how to go about the process of change. In chapter 3 you will find a general framework built on what is known about how change happens. Then, as you learn about the specific skills and methods in the ensuing chapters, you will be better able to determine not only *what* you want to change but how to do so.

Chapter 3

EXCELLING ESSENTIALS

Nothing is ours outright as a gift ...
All we are given is possibilities—
to make ourselves one thing or another.

—José Ortega y Gasset

Making changes in yourself can be easier than you expect—provided you know how to go about it. The smart way to tackle any changes in how you manage the often competing demands of your career with your personal needs is to use the proven strategies presented in this chapter.

The Skill-Building Mind-set

Research on the development of expert performance[44] dispels a widely held view that natural talent is what matters most. Instead, our understanding is that those who work at building the skills that serve as building blocks for successful behavior can level the playing field. This *skill-building* mind-set is essential to your success.

The extensive research of K. Anders Ericsson[45] shows that natural talent is traditionally overrated and oversimplified, while the role of acquired skills in the pursuit of high levels of achievement is minimized. His studies show that expert performance is a result of *skill acquisition*—the outcome of gradual improvements from extended practice (usually a minimum of ten years) within a specific area.

Further, the improvements do not come automatically from continued experience. Rather, *consistent* improvements in performance are a function of seeking out particular kinds of experiences—*deliberate practice*—that are designed to improve a particular aspect of performance. The deliberate practice requires active *reflection* to learn from each attempt what is working and what needs to be improved.

The research shows that the achievement of greatness requires ongoing *support and guidance* from experts, as well as certain nonspecific components that are likely to be present in those who become great.

One of these, as expected, is the *resolve* to stick with the process of developing expertie.

While researchers acknowledge that inherited factors and natural talent do play a role in excellence, these mostly affect what we choose *not* to do rather than what we move toward. So, for example, people small in stature do not generally seek to be defensive linemen on professional football teams.

The critical reality is that we are not hostage to some naturally granted level of talent. We can make ourselves what we will.

—Geoffrey Colvin 2006

Yet even in these sorts of choices, there are notable exceptions. There have been world-class chess masters with IQs lower than one hundred!

What are the implications of Ericsson's research for you and how you use this book? The skills that will enable you to function well in business and in the business of life can be learned. This becomes apparent once you break your performance into component skills.

A few examples include conducting meetings, analyzing and synthesizing complex economic information, maintaining a clear focus in the midst of multiple competing pressures, being mindful of how you interact with people so you can improve cooperation, managing your emotions and your nutritional needs, and so forth. Each of these requires skills that need to be refined in order to excel at *how* you deal with them.

It is notable that Ericsson's research shows a key quality of those who achieve *exceptional* success is that they continue to improve over the course of their career. In contrast, most people make great gains early on, reach a plateau, and then level off.

One of the crucial implications of this research is the importance that you focus your attention on what you can *do*, the actions you can take (including your thoughts) when dealing with the pressures you encounter. When you are precise about what you are attempting to do, you can leverage your efforts and learn to function more effectively.

Once you adopt a skill-building approach, the focus changes from you as a person to your ability to take measured actions. This viewpoint considerably reduces the angst that often happens while developing new skills, because it shifts your focus from a negative to a positive one. Rather than the negative self-statements that sometimes bog us down ("I am just no good at this"), you redirect your energy toward accomplishing your goals ("I am learning a new skill that will allow me to handle these types of situations more effectively, and this is an opportunity to practice").

The guidelines in this and the following chapters will serve as roadmaps as you seek mastery of each skill and strategy. For you to succeed, you must use deliberate practice to discover what works for you.

One of your allies in this process is the skill-building mind-set. It encourages you to think beyond the specific content of the work you need to accomplish each day, and instead focus on *how* you are getting the work done. This hardy attitude provides a key benefit: it buffers feelings of distress. It puts you in charge by leading you to ask, "Where in the midst of any difficulty is the opportunity? What can be learned? What is the aspect of it that I can get better at handling?"

Think Long Term

The skill-building mind-set also promotes the acquisition of the skills that lay the foundation for your capacity to achieve your good life. The more reliable and habitual your self-management skills become, the more easily you will move toward your goals. With sufficient practice, you can expect that when you are under a strain, your automatic fallback coping strategies will be the ones that enhance your capacity to operate in your ideal executive performance state.

It was once believed that our brains become fixed after a certain (young) age. The research on brain plasticity (*neuroplasticity*)[46] now shows that the brain can continue to be malleable throughout life. It has the capacity to reorganize neural pathways when exposed to new experiences. When we acquire new knowledge and skills, these show up as structural and functional changes in the brain. This is critically important because it means you can expect the changes you set in motion now to become more ingrained, automatic, and effortless over time.

Let's review a few important facts to know about making changes.

Self-Improvement Essentials

Those who do not understand the process of change tend to seek unrealistic changes, seek realistic changes in unrealistic ways, and unnecessarily accept resignation as a fact of life.[47] The information below provides the key components of the smart way go about self-improvement.[48] It is best to combine these with the Make It Happen section at the end of most of the chapters in the book to help you apply these guidelines to the specific skills.

Whatever else is going on in your life, you will derive deep satisfaction from continuing to grow and master the challenges of your life.

Give Change a Chance

The general timeline to develop a new simple habit, such as going to sleep at a specific time, is twenty-one continuous days of practice. More complex processes, such as those encompassed by the term "executive wisdom," can take as long as ten years to develop.[49] I strongly recommend you start with a one-month commitment. That will allow enough practice for you to discover real benefits without overwhelming yourself by looking too far off into the horizon.

Adapt a Change Mind-set

The critical elements of the mind-set you should bring to the process of self-improvement are shown here in figure 3.1.

Mind-set for Change

Commitment—Your resolve is a critical ingredient for success in making a change.

Purpose—To sustain your resolve, engage the deep sense of purpose that arises from your goals of fulfillment, security, and personal power.

Persistence—To stick with the process of change, you must maintain your efforts by holding on to a skill-building perspective.

Strong Will—Your will—self-discipline and perseverance—*is your true ally* in sustaining effort.

Expectation of Resistance to Change—Use a strategy that *gradually* shifts you into a new set point to offset the natural tendency for the mind-body to maintain equilibrium by sticking to the familiar.

Figure 3.1

Commitment. Your *readiness to change* is the crucial ingredient to your success. That means that you are finished contemplating the matter and have made a decision to invest in the change. Leading researchers[50] in behavioral change report that people who actually make a *resolution to change* are ten times more likely to succeed in changing their behavior than those who don't.

Purpose. Your power to sustain your resolution derives from the extent to which it is based upon a deep sense of purpose. Ideally, you believe it is instrumental to your fulfillment, security, or personal power.

Persistence. Those who approach habit change as a training process rather than a single event do better. Taking the long view will keep you progressing toward mastery. Change is rarely as straightforward or easy as you might at first expect.[51] Each day you must make the decision to continue building your new patterns.

Expectation of Resistance to Change. The mind-body's tendency to maintain homeostasis is such that it will resist your efforts to make changes. At its best, homeostasis serves to regulate physiological balance, such as body temperature and blood sugar levels, in order to maintain optimum functioning. It also regulates our brain and behavior. It works beautifully most of the time.

The problem is, like a boat's autopilot, it tries to hold to a course even if set by factors that are no longer applicable. Our mind-body system perceives significant change as a threat, and so it tries to reestablish equilibrium by returning to what is

> *Discipline is the guardrail that keeps you on the path of self-esteem.*
>
> —Kent Nelson

familiar. When this happens, the system sends out alarm signals, like physical discomfort or emotional upset, that make returning to the normal set point—the familiar—very appealing. To make changes, you must *retrain* your mind-body system and thereby reset your comfort zone until the new behavior is the norm. You must stay on manual control, making slow steady steps to ease yourself into the new patterns, until your mind-body recognizes them as normal. It takes a minimum, some believe, of sixty-six days to maintain the changes on autopilot.

Managing Setbacks. Studies[52] show that believing in your ability to make and sustain changes—self-efficacy—correlates with success, so it is important your strategies include constructively dealing with moments of weakness or setbacks, rather than allowing them to become full-blown relapses. People who give up along the way often do so because they view a relapse as evidence that they don't have what it takes to make changes. Search instead for the situational causes that temporarily set you back and learn from them as you resume your efforts.

Your Action Plan

Once you are committed to making an improvement, you must take action for real change to happen. To get the greatest return on your efforts, you need a well-conceived and designed strategic plan. Use your vision of the good life that you created in chapter 2 to make your own action plan. The Action Plan Template (see figure 3.2) incorporates the research on the smart way to make changes. It will help you to focus your efforts. What follows is a brief explanation of the action steps on the template.

Identify What Needs to Change

What is it that you want to change? When you envisioned your *good life* and reflected on where you are right now in relation to that vision (see chapter 2), you set in motion a process that you can use to identify what you need to change to reach your goals. As you read on, you may find you gain further clarity about the challenges you are facing and the skills that will help you meet them as you create the synergy you need for success. You may want to revise your action plan accordingly.

Identify Benefits of Change

While there may be external incentives, such as a performance evaluation, that are influencing your decision to make a change, the more you feel a strong personal incentive the better. Clarify what makes achieving this outcome important to you. What benefits do you expect from this change?

To make your action more compelling, write a few sentences on the benefits you expect in each of the following key areas, and any others that matter to you. Be as specific and detailed as you can, using the following guidelines.

Work Performance—mental and physical energy, focus, concentration, determination, creativity, flexibility, consistency, productivity, attitude toward challenges, job satisfaction

Work Relationships—composure, emotional resilience, confidence, good listener, empathy, respectful, considerate, openness, team player, cooperative, nonthreatening, friendly, comfortable, sense of humor, healthy boundaries

Personal Relationships—able to let go of work, capacity to be fully present with important others; absence of irritability from residuals of work stress, empathy, respectful, considerate, openness, playfulness, intimacy

Personal life—capacity to let go of work and shift gears so you can feel lighter, more relaxed, and be more playful; enjoy hobbies, recreational activities, be with family and friends in satisfying ways

Well-Being—self-esteem; hardiness; sleep; eating; physical and mental health; reduction in frequency and intensity of being overloaded or distressed, stress-related symptoms, abuse of substances

Identify the Consequences of Not Changing

What are the costs of the way you are handling this skill now? Be sure to include "hidden costs," such as chronic stress, poor energy, interpersonal tensions, and dissatisfaction with work.

What will be the cost if you continue the path you are on? What is the worst case scenario you see if you choose to do nothing about this skill? Describe any additional consequences that have special meaning to you.

Consider the five key areas identified above to focus your attention and to do an honest self-appraisal.

Action Plan Template

I. Identify what needs to change

What needs to change in order for you to create your version of the good life?

II. Identify benefits of change

Work Performance

Work Relationships

Personal Relationships

Personal Life

Well-Being

III. Identify consequences of not changing

Current Costs

Projected Long-Term Costs

Worst-Case Scenario

IV. Identify essential components of change

- specific steps you will take
- resources you need
- identify allies
- methods for tracking progress
- strategies for sustaining progress
- specific observable indicators of achievement

V. Create your action plan

Create a timeline and designate times for specific actions.

Maintain a progress log.

Enlist someone to hold you accountable.

Muster personal support.

Appreciate progress.

VI. Review these guidelines.

Figure 3.2

Identify the Essential Components of Change

The questions outlined below cover essential dimensions of a viable action plan. Add other elements that are important to your unique situation, if needed.

- What are the specific steps that you will need to take to make this improvement happen? Are there specific skills that you need to strengthen in order to bring about the changes that you envision? If so, what are the steps that you will take to acquire those skills?
- What resources do you need (schedule adjustments, people to absorb some of your usual duties)? What guidelines will you use to focus your efforts? What were the key elements in prior successful efforts at self-improvement? How much time will you need to devote to the process each day and week?
- Who are your allies? How will you enlist them to support your efforts? Who will hold you accountable? To whom can you delegate tasks so that you have the time you need to devote to this matter? Who will listen to your frustrations and joys?
- How will you track progress? What are the specific measures of action that you will track? How often will you record and review these actions?
- How will you sustain progress? How will you connect with your intention each day and week? How will you deal with setbacks and discouragement? How will you reward progress?
- How will you know when you have achieved your goal? What are the specific observable indicators?

Create Your Action Plan

Create A Timeline and Designate Times for Specific Tasks. Determine your start date and goal date, and then map your component steps onto the schedule. Be realistic about the timeline for your efforts to build new skills. While you don't want to set yourself up for failure by trying to short cut the process, it is critical to commit to specific steps on a timeline rather than leaving it open-ended. Too often, people approach a new task by saying, "I'll do it when I find the time."

Experience shows you must make time to take the intended action. So be specific about how will you modify your schedule and your priorities to do the work needed for this change.

Review and revise your timeline as needed.

Maintain a Log. An effective way to monitor progress and to stay honest about your commitment is to keep a record of key actions. Make entries of what you did, including observations of what is working or not, at the time of the action.

Enlist Someone to Hold You Accountable. Even the most self-directed people will periodically drift off course. Arrange for someone to check with you at least once a week to provide a nudge to stick with the process.

Muster Personal Support. Research shows that support from others can make the process go better—a *lot* better—when you have the right support and encouragement for sustaining the effort. One way to stay on top of this issue is to schedule a regular time each week to share how things are going with your life partner or a good friend.

Be attentive to your support team. Be sure they know your goals, some of the glitches you expect to encounter, and show appreciation for their input and any strain your agenda may cause them.

Appreciate Progress. At the end of each week, step back and review how things went. Identify what worked and what did not. Make changes, as needed, in order to maximize success in meeting weekly goals.

Learn to appreciate the often small but meaningful improvements to aid your persistence. The concept of the *private victory*, popularized by Stephen Covey,[53] refers to the personal meaning of both large and small achievements.

There is another kind of progress that is a crucial part of the change process—the small improvements in *how* you did something. The changes you notice may be relatively small, perhaps a change that nobody else would even notice or appreciate. For example, when working on your demeanor while dealing with an annoying staff member, your private victory might be a feeling of being slightly less irritated or more quickly remembering to take a calming breath before speaking to this person.

A useful way of referring to these small changes comes from the concept of a Just Noticeable Difference (JND). Drawn from psychophysiological research, this is a way to measure small shifts in awareness. For example, in studies that sought to determine differences in skin sensitivity in various locations on the body, researchers used a wooden fork-like device with two moveable prongs to press against the subject's skin. Small changes in the distance between the fork's prongs were not noticeable. As the distance increased, there came a point when the subject started to notice that the one point of pressure became two. The JND is the subjective recognition of a difference that enables the subject to recognize that a change has happened. Appreciating JNDs in one's own behavior is a vital part of building your capacity to stick with making larger changes.

Because appreciating JNDs can be a vital part of sustaining the effort to stick with making larger changes, it is prudent to plan times to reflect on your private victories. An effective way to do this is to take a couple of minutes at the end of each day to identify three successes. The regular use of daily affirmations also fosters the expectation that you will be reviewing your private victories at the end of the day, which will increase your tendency to take the actions during the day.

Review These Guidelines

You can enhance your success and develop confidence in your capacity for self-improvement by periodically reviewing the guidelines in this chapter. If you get stuck, that simply means that you need to reconsider your plan and add or change elements that will allow you to reach your goals. By systematically recording your observations you have a working document that you can use when making other changes.[54]

~.~.~.~.~.~.~.~.~.~.~.~.~.~.~.~.~.~.~.~

Make It Happen

Step One. At this early phase of making self-improvements, you need to rough out your first action plan. Write down your goals and your plan now to make the process more real than if you just continue contemplating change. Use the action plan template, included above or downloadable at www.mhkcoaching.com. You can make changes, as needed, as you read further in the book.

Step Two. Take action now on the one component in your action plan (see figure 3.2) that will set the hook in your commitment to the self-improvement process (see Identify the Essential Components of Change). This step makes your commitment real, which activates the process of change. In the least, it starts you getting acclimated to the idea that certain specific things are going to happen.

Step Three. Identify someone you trust and get that person involved. Even if you are disinclined to share your ruminations with others, it is prudent to push yourself to do so. You will derive energy from others to stick with the process by having them enquire about your progress over time. You can have more control over how this goes by requesting that your support person checks with you on a regular basis and in a specific way that you find helpful.

Section III
ESSENTIALS OF PEAK PERFORMANCE

Introduction

Problems cannot be solved at the same level of perspective
from which they are perceived to exist as problems.
That only repeats the error.
Some new level of perspective must be found.

—Albert Einstein

Some years ago, a young Barred Owl got stuck in our chimney. Perplexed with how to liberate it, I called people who I thought would be the experts. The local wildlife sanctuary suggested using a chimney brush to push the owl down to the bottom, where I could capture and release it. Fortunately, before I had time to try that method, I spoke with someone who really understood the nature of birds—a falconer. If I had followed the advice of the wildlife sanctuary, he said, the owl would have resisted my efforts by flapping its wings, and I would have broken those outspread wings by pushing down with the brush! He suggested instead that I drop a thick rope down the chimney and then make some noise at the bottom to scare the bird. Owls are powerful climbers, he explained. In its efforts to get away from the noise, the owl would dig its talons into the rope, climb up out of the chimney, and fly away. It worked marvelously well. Within seconds, we heard the young bird and several other Barred Owls cackling loudly as they reunited.

Your efforts to improve your performance and to increase your satisfaction in life will go much better too when you understand and align your strategies with your true human nature and unique personality, values, needs, beliefs, styles, strengths and limitations. Alas, getting that alignment—the acquisition of self-wisdom—is not easy. It requires you to successfully navigate some pitfalls that are described in this section.

An Integrated System

In section III, you will find a user-friendly framework for understanding how our core system works. This section offers efficient and effective methods to optimize your functioning. The focus is on methods to self-regulate your mind-body system as a foundation for building your personal success equation. The criteria for inclusion in the guidelines is that the methods must:

- be dependable,
- be sustainable,
- be nonintrusive,
- require little effort.

These methods must work quietly in the background, like a good computer operating system, so you can be free to devote your best energy to other aspects of your career. The overall goal is to develop an integrated lifestyle that supports *your* performance needs. Just a little time up front, including the deliberate practice of methods, will allow these methods to become well-honed routines and rituals.

The CEO Stress Project Findings and You

The CEO Stress Project findings confirmed that seasoned, successful executives are deeply invested in performing optimally each day. The participants described their own clear imperative that they bring their ideal executive performance state to the challenges and opportunities of the day and maintain this state over the long haul. Further, the participants recognized the risk of weaknesses in their capacity to manage the ongoing strain of their jobs: increased likelihood of performance deficits due to fatigue, interpersonal tensions, illness, and missed workdays.

Most of these successful executive do not get tripped up by distress because their intolerance for functioning poorly makes them eager to find what works. They continually seek better ways to manage the pressures and are open to new ideas, not getting caught up in shortsighted self-esteem issues that might lead them to reject new and improved strategies. Quick to move into a proactive stance, they described effective stress management as a set of essential skills that they strive to improve.

In fact, many of these executives were so skilled at managing their own pressures and operated so automatically, that it was an interesting challenge to get them to be explicit about what happens when they *do* have difficulties. For example, I'd challenge them by asking, "And when that doesn't work, what then?" By hearing more about their worst-case scenarios, I was able to learn about instances when they do lose their cool. This allowed me to identify their fall-back strategies which are described throughout the book.

Virtually all of the executives acknowledged the importance of self-care, such as rest, nutrition, sleep, and exercise. Yet many were candid about the fact that they are not as consistent about some elements of caring for themselves as they know they should be. Only a few were formally trained in relaxation methods, though they have other ways of calming themselves, as you will read in anecdotes in the chapters that follow.

Your efforts to deliberately learn the methods outlined in the book can put you on an equal footing with admired CEOs as you develop your own ways of handling the executive hot seat.

Overview of Section III

The eight chapters in Section III provide the essential framework for understanding how the mind-body operates, what it needs to function optimally, and the simplest yet most powerful methods for managing your system. The objective is that the individual components will work together to offer you Synergy for Success. By effectively managing these core needs, your operating system will be best equipped to successfully meet the challenges of the daily grind (described in section IV).

Chapter 4, Maintaining a Cool Operating System, explains how your basic operating system works and the key elements it requires to function optimally.

Chapter 5, Regulating Your Operating System, explains the biopsychological imperatives and the immediate practical implications with simple, easy-to-learn guidelines for self-regulation.

Chapter 6, Managing A Personal Energy Crisis, outlines the role of energy that fuels your biopsychological system. Guidelines are provided for monitoring the status of your system and for mobilizing and sustaining good energy.

Chapter 7, Making Every Day Great, integrates the ways you can use your mind with specific methods to take control of key aspects of the workday.

Chapter 8, The Myth of Multitasking, provides specific guidelines to help you gain the power of focus.

Chapter 9, Renewing Yourself, offers methods that address the crucial need for revitalizing your mind, body, and spirit.

Chapter 10, Executive Cool, lays out methods to foster stability and resiliency in the face of challenges so you can maintain your ideal executive performance state.

Chapter 11, Recovery from Loss of Cool, addresses those inevitable occasions when the pressures of the day throw you off kilter. It provides efficient, reliable, and powerful methods for regaining your cool.

Chapter 4

MAINTAINING A COOL OPERATING SYSTEM

If you want to thrive in the twenty-first century,
you need to have internal hardiness resources to manage workplace stress.

—S. R. Maddi and D. M. Khoshaba, *Resilience at Work*

To meet your evolving career demands you need a reliable, well-tuned, high-performance mind-body operating system. You also need to have good physical and mental energy. Fortunately, when all parts of your system are functioning well and are synchronized, you gain energy from the synergy. This is when your operating system is functioning in cool mode and you are performing in your ideal executive performance state.

This chapter provides an overview of the general principles and guidelines to manage your system, using the Hardiness for Hard Times approach. This decidedly hands-on strategy *requires* that you know your system's capabilities and requirements, and develop basic self-management methods to keep it performing optimally. The science of human performance offers a clear imperative for attending to the roles of both mind and body as they work together in synchrony, hence the term mind-body. Nonetheless, many executives operate as if they could separate the two, generally giving priority to the thinking part of their system and neglecting their bodies.

Your Mind-Body at Work

Jules Feiffer's cartoon aside, your basic sense of yourself resides within your mind-body—an integrated biopsychological system. When your health is good, your mind is clear and sharp, and the matters of your daily life are going well, you take your system for granted. You probably treat your system as you do your computer—you pay little attention to it as long as it's working well. When it is not functioning well, you give it to a tech expert so they can optimize its performance. It is not that easy with your mind-body operating system. You have some basic responsibilities. Your system needs you to manage it!

You will find the process of learning how to manage this system easier when you shift from a self-focused perspective to an objective one. A common self-statement when someone perceives something is out of kilter in his or her system might be, "There is something wrong with me." Think about the mind shift that happens when you say, instead, "Something is out of alignment with the workings of my mind-body." This mind-set helps offset the normal tendency to react to shortcomings as a personal matter, such as, "I have a character flaw or an inherent deficiency." Then you can more readily focus on a problem-solving approach, such as, "My mind is doing 'X' and my body is doing 'Z.' What can I do about that?"

Think of yourself as an orchestra conductor monitoring all the parts of the orchestra to determine how each section is contributing to the overall harmony and quality of the music. Sometimes you signal one section to modify its intensity or pace to enhance the orchestra's performance. You may need to call a rehearsal where you can stop the orchestra, temporarily focus on a specific section to improve its tone or rhythm, and then bring all the pieces back together.

Your mind-body needs you to manage it!

Similarly, self-management skills involve monitoring and regulating key aspects of your own system. The following working model of the mind-body operating system provides the basic rationale you need. It simplifies the basics you will need to *intentionally* override your *automatic* tendency to ignore the communications from your brain-body system. This lays the groundwork for maintaining your ideal executive performance state.

Mind-Body Basics

As noted earlier, we often think of the brain and body as separate entities, even though they are intertwined components of a complex integrated system, like the software and hardware of your computer. It is sometimes useful to look at the unique characteristics of each, because their distinctive capacities, limitations, and default modes govern the modifications we can make. However, in this chapter, we focus on the way the two systems are wired together in order to lay a foundation for better management of your own system. Rest assured you don't have to become a software expert or a psychologist. However, you do need a working understanding of how your brain and body work to leverage your efforts to manage stress.

The Biopsychological Imperative

The mind-body system is designed to maintain itself (homeostasis) and thrive as it encounters the demands for action in life. Any call to action is a *stressor*, because it puts pressure on the system to expend energy. The greater the demand for energy, the more it throws our system out of balance. The *stress response* is the natural attempt of your system to mobilize the energy needed to restore balance. It is activated in the lower part of the brain stem, just as in nonthinking animals. It causes the secretion of stress hormones that activate the parts of the nervous system to be ready to fight with or flee from the threat. It is *not* inherently mediated by the conscious mind. It is designed that way because when a real threat is present, you often do not have time to think. You need your reactions to be fast and efficient.

In his book *Why Zebras Don't Get Ulcers*, neurobiologist Robert M. Sapolsky[55] notes that the key difference between zebras and humans is that the zebra's stress response only happens when the threat, like an approaching lion, is actually present. Once the threat is gone, the system returns to quiescence. Because humans *think*, all we have to do is imagine the lion and our fight-flight reaction gets triggered. Furthermore, our higher brain functions also mean the stress response is part of a more complex general adaptation syndrome—we are reactive to a whole array of stressors, not just physical threats. Social and psychological stressors,

51

as well as the anticipation of these, trigger our stress response. Our stress reaction can thereby easily and frequently get triggered.

What you likely refer to as being "stressed" is, in fact, the experience of *distress*—when the stress response is being triggered to such an extent that the demands for *energy* are exceeding your system's capacity to respond effectively. The sense of distress is actually secondary to the experience of *effort*.

You may have noticed that as you draw down your store of energy, everything you do begins to feel more effortful. You begin to feel like you are working harder to accomplish tasks that generally feel easy. A closer look will help you understand what is happening so that you will have a better understanding of what you need to do to manage this natural process.

Natural Performance Rhythms

There was a time that scientists' prevailing view was that we humans only had two cycles, wake and sleep, called circadian rhythms. We now know that there are numerous daily fluctuations (see figure 4.1) built into our "operating systems," and these are referred to as ultradian rhythms.

Psychologist Ernest Rossi[56] explains that *regardless of the source of the demands* for your energy, your ability to perform well at any given moment is intimately tied to where you are in your cycle of energy depletion and recovery. The bottom line is that your system can sustain high levels of performance for only ninety minutes! Then it needs to recover energy to prepare for the next high-energy performance period.

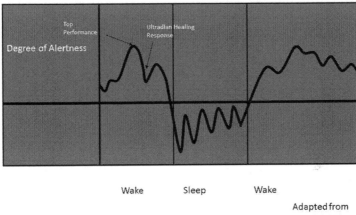

Figure 4.1

The fluctuations of natural energy rhythms affect your performance over the course of the day as shown in figure 4.2. You can override them by force of will, for example by riding the stimulation of high pressure meetings or by giving your system an extra charge from caffeine. However, when you override your natural rhythms, there are costs.

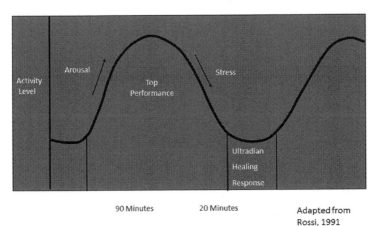

Figure 4.2

53

Short-term Costs. Rossi points out that when you reject the mind-body's natural need for energy recovery, it then takes more effort to produce results. The more you push, the more you cause stress and the more you wear down your system. In most cases, your resiliency allows you to absorb this distress periodically. The problems occur when it persists

Midterm Costs. When you continue to reject nature's call for recovery you are heading for burnout (note small "b"), like a battery running low on charge. The *stress messenger*—the signals from (a) your mind, such as fretting, (b) your body, such as tension, and (c) your performance—are telling you you're mentally, physically, or spiritually straining and in need of recovery. You then increasingly find yourself in "malfunction junction," where numerous mistakes creep into your performance, memory, and learning. This is when emotional and interpersonal problems also become apparent (see figure 4.3).

Breakdowns Due to Lack of Energy

- accident proneness and clumsiness
- judgment errors and bad decisions despite knowing better
- repeated errors in spelling, typing, and computing
- significant memory problems, like forgetting what you were saying or looking for
- slips of the tongue, such as misspeaking; using wrong words
- missing important implications in conversations and failing to understand puns and jokes
- social miscues and gaffes

Adapted from Rossi 1991

Figure 4.3

Long-term Costs. Unless you build in effective ways to respond to your needs, the demands of being a CEO can lead to a situation in which your operating system is on a continual alert status. It feels good to be "pumped up," which makes it easy to become addicted to the "high." However, with the heightened sense of readiness comes a steady flow of stress hormones (such as cortisol and epinephrine), which can result in psychological and medical problems. You may find yourself feeling progressively weary and notice increasingly intrusive demands for relief. The result? Your performance wanes, anxiety, depression and insomnia increase, and your ambition is relegated to the backseat. Desperate for relief, you become susceptible to "stealing" recovery by the overuse of food, alcohol, sexual outlets and chemical substances (including an overreliance on prescribed medicines). If you continue to push yourself, you are likely to reach a point of emotional and spiritual burnout, like a battery that cannot be recharged. No amount of pep talking or caffeine will help.

Sapolsky[57] describes the downstream effect over time from continually bathing your body in stress hormones. There is an accumulation of physical damage that lays the foundation for maladies such as high blood pressure, headaches, muscle pain, irritable bowel syndrome, heart disease, and cancer.

Why does your system operate this way? Wouldn't it be more adaptive from an evolutionary perspective to be able to work for an infinite length of time and to have unlimited stores of energy? Interestingly, psychologists Stephen Kaplan and Marc Berman[58] provide a compelling hypothesis for the adaptive value of limited resources and the experience of *effort* that increases when a person attempts to persist on a task: it serves as "an inducement to back off if possible, thus reducing further depletion the important resource."[59] It also *protects us* from the hazards caused by neglecting other important matters in our lives.

> *Self-control is a complex, biologically expensive form of behavior.*
> —Baumeister, Vohs, and Tice 2007

The take-away message for the average person may be that he can have a better life if he manages his energy well. However, when you aspire to function optimally as a CEO, you cannot be content merely to conserve energy. You need to be sure that you have good ongoing energy for the expected demands, as well as the energy reserves for unexpected high demand events. For that, you need a better grasp of how your mind-body system uses energy and strategies to work with your system to optimize its performance.

Energy and Mental Performance: the Science

There is an extensive body of research on the complex interplay between energy and mental performance. One group of studies[60] examined the effect of two different types of self-control tasks that deplete mental energy. The first type of task required *attention regulation*: participants were instructed to watch a video of someone being interviewed and to ignore extraneous stimuli such as words that appeared at the bottom of the screen. The second type of task required *emotion control*: participants were told to watch an emotionally charged movie but to suppress their emotional responses.

After performing those tasks, participants were asked to perform a number of other tasks that varied in type and degree of mental complexity (from the simple recall of information to constructing mental models and making inferences based on a set of postulates). Their performance on these follow-up tasks was compared to two groups without the special instructions. The scientist found that *directed attention* depletes energy such that performance on a complex task that follows suffers. The broad implication noted by these psychologists is that our higher mental "powers are fragile in that these cognitive abilities are reduced when resources are depleted."[61]

If the challenges of being a CEO were as simple as they are for college students participating in a laboratory experiment, managing your energy would be comparatively simple. However, studies[62] in neuropsychology showed that the self-control required by the kind of demands you face every day as a CEO, such as higher order mental skills and more basic emotional regulation, all *draw on the same pool of energy*. This means that as you draw on the energy needed for tasks such as planning and organizing, you are depleting the *same energy resource* that you need for more basic self-regulation, such as the ability to inhibit impulses, maintain flexibility, and control your emotions—to stay cool.

Furthermore, the areas of executive mental functioning overlap and must work together to bring about *smooth functioning*. Therefore, a weakness in one aspect of executive functioning affects other related ones, as well as the more advanced processes built on these skills. For example, good time management requires planning as well as self-monitoring. That means that a weak ability in a single component of executive mental skills will compromise the overall effectiveness of mental functioning. This is true whether the weakness is due to an inherent executive function problem (as seen in people with ADD, for example), or other factors, such as being overloaded.

The mandate is clear: to perform optimally as a CEO you must be good at managing your energy. With this research foundation, you can see why high-level executives are sometimes referred to as "white-collar athletes."[63] In fact, your job is even harder in some respects than that of a professional athlete. Your performance demands you to be "on" almost all the time, whereas athletes get breaks between events. Furthermore, you are more like a decathlete because of the multiple types of skills and abilities that are required. Like the training for an athlete, your performance depends on a systematic and thoughtful approach to managing yourself and regulating your energy.

Managing Energy the Hardy Way

The Hardiness for Hard Times approach to managing energy requires that *you are the CEO of you!*

You must apply *self-management* methods to regulate the demands on your energy (for example, setting realistic goals, improving skills, and managing pressures put on you), and *self-care* methods to provide the needed energy (e.g., eating, resting, and recreation). You will learn strategies that allow you to synchronize your efforts with the rhythmic needs of your mind-body operating system. Then, as described by Jim Loehr and Tony Schwartz, you can reliably bring *The Power of Full Engagement*[64] to the pressures you encounter.

Sound daunting? As you contemplate the real-world application of these ideal goals to your life, be sure to keep the following key points in mind.

(1) Much of what you will learn builds on what you already know and do. The guidelines I offer in this book will help you refine that in order to bring about enhanced performance.

(2) It is natural to be drawn to short-term fixes rather than stick with making longer-term lifestyle changes. When you disrupt that tendency, you undertake an ongoing process that will bring continued refinements and satisfaction over the course of your career.

(3) As with any effort to improve skills, mastery and ease are the payoff for an initial sense of clumsiness and encumbrance. Deliberate practice brings automaticity, and with it comes improved long-term performance and lasting satisfaction.

(4) It is important that any time you hit a stumbling block you review the proven guidelines for making change presented

in chapter 3.[65] Pay particular attention to the importance of making and appreciating small steady steps.

Regulating Energy

Managing your energy entails the three interrelated components depicted in (figure 4.3): *monitoring* the "data" of your mind, body, and emotions; *processing* the data through the three "filters "of your logical mind, your other-than-rational mind, and with another person; and taking *action* that reduces the demand for energy and/or increases recovery of energy.

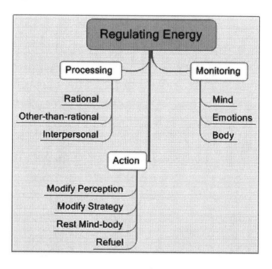

Figure 4.3

Monitoring

You already monitor some energy resources, like the charge on your cell phone and access to food. You have established routines to take care of those matters. However, with all the competing demands for your energy, the best way to improve the effectiveness of your monitoring is by using systematic routines.

The two types of routines that will assure accuracy are self-monitoring and monitoring by someone else. The objective is that your methods enable you to achieve a reliable comfortable rhythm and smoothness in the ways you manage your energy. Remember, monitoring just gives you information. Nevertheless, the effect of being more aware is that you are more likely to be mobilized to take constructive action at an advantageous point.

Self-Monitoring. The personal positioning system (PPS), introduced in chapter 2, provides a model you can adapt for yourself. Periodic refinements will be necessary as your circumstances change. Your PPS should function like a robust GPS that provides the specific information you need about where you are in relation to current and pending demands for energy and status of energy resources. Since no single integrated PPS software application is currently available you will need to create the combination of methods that work for you. I recommend you use a robust mind-mapping program as a key component of your PPS. It should give you a graphic image of your matters of concerns, which you can expand into subcomponents and collapse to narrow your perspective.

A good place to start is to have a visual representation, like the one in figure 4.4 that displays an overview of the categories your PPS should monitor. A sample breakdown into subcategories of matters of concern that require energy appears in figure 4.5. Subsequent chapters will provide guidelines for monitoring at more specific levels.

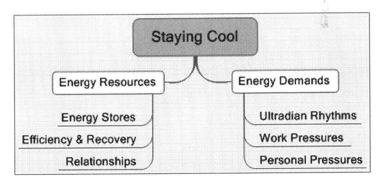

Figure 4.4

A weekly review of your main areas of concern is generally the minimum required to hold yourself accountable for each. A key objective is that you can address each area sufficiently so when you need to focus your attention on another matter, you are free from the drain on your energy of any matters that have not been adequately addressed.

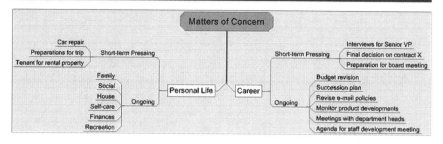

Figure 4.5

There are two simple and easy ways to improve your monitoring capability. One is to use the Personal Asset Allocations template (see chapter 2) to get a general sense of how your energy resources are affecting your performance. Be sure to modify it to reflect the ideal and minimum levels for each that you require to perform well and to move your life in the direction of your most important goals.[66] The second is a simple log in which you keep track (ratings on a scale of 1 to 10) of how well you are meeting your needs such as sleep, nourishment, social support and recreation. If you prefer a visual log, make a pie chart and shade in how well you are doing in each area.

There is one caveat to factor into your monitoring system. Nobody can be on top of everything all the time, yet our default operating system is governed by the biopsychological imperative: any *call to action* is a *stressor* because it puts pressure on you to expend energy. Consequently, when you are making sense of the pressures you face, you need to keep in mind that even when you are not consciously aware of feeling pressured by a matter of concern, it may be causing a drain on your energy.

To take charge of such potential energy drains, it is best to have systematic ways to call your attention to them. For example, you might identify any matters that you are prone to glossing over or missing altogether and have a checklist and a set of questions to ask yourself about each. Or you may appoint someone else to hold you accountable (see monitoring by somebody directly below). The added structure and resulting monitoring can enable you to take ownership for each, which gives you more choice over how and when you choose to deal with the pressure. The ideal is that you can have more energy to deal with matters that you determine are important rather than ones that become important because you have neglected them. To put effort into this strategy you have to value peace of mind as an overriding quality of your life, as well as appreciate the value of having it so that you can fully immerse yourself in another that you choose to engage. In doing so, you are also fostering synergy amongst the various aspects of your life.

Monitoring by Somebody. Because we all have blind spots and can slip into phases when we are dominated by one pressure at the expense of others, it is prudent to develop a *buddy system*. SCUBA divers and military troops require the use of a buddy relationship to provide a nearly failsafe method for mutual protection. SCUBA divers have a structured routine they follow before their dive to check equipment, agree on signals, and to plan the dive. After the dive, they review how it went.

An effective way to build structure and accountability with your buddy[67] is to have a weekly thirty-minute meeting where you each get half the time to review your weekly agenda, any notable concerns, and progress. Informal but routine exchanges with your buddy can also serve to mutually monitor how things are going.

You may want to designate one buddy at work and another in your personal life to assure that you are being monitored by people who care in both domains. Authorize each to "watch your back." You want them to let you know when they see the "red flags" that you have identified as signs that you are drifting off course or are operating in a deficit mode. For example, your buddy will let you know when you are focusing too much on a matter that is distracting you from your more important goals, and if you appear tired, are having trouble concentrating, or being irritable.

The regular monitoring you do with each other also provides a special opportunity for you each to express your appreciation of the other's efforts and private victories!

Processing

The activity of processing is like triaging in a medical setting. In the present context, it means filtering your observations about the demands for energy and status of energy resources and sorting them into a plan of action to provide the energy needed.

The actual mental-emotional method of doing that is sufficiently complex as to exceed the scope of this book. Instead, the focus here is on *factors that enhance your capacity to do the processing*. Of course that brings up a frequent source of frustration with psychologists: it seems everything is a process to us. In fact, we believe that understanding and working with processes is central in matters of human psychology and behavior.

We have had to deal with the frustration ourselves. It is part of human nature. In my first graduate school course in clinical psychology, my fellow students and I were eager to learn the laws of human psychology, just like the laws of physics and chemistry. Much to our chagrin, the professor's reply to our questions were invariably, "Well, it depends!" So we set about acquiring an understanding of the factors that come into play, which can alter one's psychology and behavior.

As we direct our attention to how you can manage your observations about the pressures you face and your energy resources, you will want to know the rules to follow. What I can do is provide guidelines (below) to some of the key factors that will help the activity of processing go smoother and better for you. Then, guidelines for specific strategies are provided in the chapters that follow.

Poet David Whyte's insights[68] are an invaluable source for understanding the human drama of managing ourselves as we engage work and our personal lives. He provides a particularly astute and helpful framework[69] that integrates the complexity of what you are trying to do when processing. He recommends that you view each of the main areas of your life as a *marriage* with the attendant commitments—made consciously or unconsciously—and the negotiations and struggles between them (processing) as *conversations*. Using the term marriage promotes a deeper appreciation for the forces that underlie the interactions—often an essential dimension for achieving the level of empathy and respect required to achieve the best outcomes.

Personal Processing. It is best to remember that one big factor influencing the amount of energy required to deal with any demand is the level of *skill* you bring to it. It follows that when feeling strained by pressure, one of the first factors you should consider is your proficiency in dealing with it. In this context, the term *skill* refers to how you manage yourself as well as business and interpersonal pressures.

Another central factor influencing how you process your observations is the effectiveness of your methods for *resolving competing agendas.* You must trust that your methods are sufficiently comprehensive for you to feel grounded and committed to the course of action you take. The more secure you are, the less energy it will take.

To achieve that, you will especially need to guard against any tendencies to simplify matters, which are inherently complex. In general, CEOs prefer processing matters in a linear, no-nonsense way. For many business decisions, that generally works well. However, when there are competing factors for managing demands (whether they are within the work or personal domains, or between one domain and the other), the effect is that you are feeling pulled in more than one direction. Since that can bind up energy, you must be sure you have methods that enhance the *process* of integration.

A good initial strategy is a simple structured routine for reviewing the various demands for energy (within and between the areas of work, personal, family, and social); the value you place on each; and your plans for allocating and recovering energy. This particular method of prioritizing makes it more likely you will give each aspect of your life its fair due. It can be an especially effective strategy to stay on top of your resource needs for the next few days, when the review happens at the end of one day or the start of the new one.

Using your PPS as a guide, you may find as few as ten minutes will be sufficient for a viable routine. It is important you do it as seriously as you check your folder prior to an important meeting. You will have to guard against this becoming perfunctory. To be effective, you must genuinely notice matters that need attention in the various domains of your life *and* reflect on their importance on how and when you will manage each within the context of your other pressures. The objective is that your plan eliminates the pressure from "competing" issues so you can direct your energy to the designated one.

Pausing. Interspersed with every method you use to manage your energy is the extent to which you are psychologically *centered*. In one sense, that is the focus of this book. The following terms capture nuances of what being centered means: to be true to yourself, well-grounded, self-assured, clear-headed, and to have your wits about you. This is so important that I started the book with the poem "Pausing." It eloquently describes the value of interrupting the usual mode of action so your mind-body system can have the opportunity to restore its alignment. It is in these pauses that the rush of activity gives way to the process of metabolizing the data.

Armed with your commitment to manage your personal side as well as you manage your work demands, you need ways to assure that when facing competing pressures you can reliably achieve resolutions that integrate your various values and needs. By learning to pause and to foster being centered, you gain an effect that is similar to how a gyroscope helps a ship or airplane maintain stability when it encounters cross-currents and winds.

While any pause can be beneficial, there are some methods[70] that, especially when done regularly, will give you the greatest ROI (return on investment) in your efforts to manage competing pressures. These methods help you disengage from the usual pressures and from the purely rationale approach so the other-than-rational elements can emerge and be part of the processing. That is what often happens naturally when you are in the shower, walking the dog, or enjoying vacation.

The value of using these methods is that you make certain you are regularly getting the benefits. Of course you can also use any of these for a targeted purpose, like when you know you are feeling entangled by competing pressures.

I encourage you to try out the various structured methods for pausing described below. While it is possible to use books and other media guides for each of these practices, they do not offer the individualized monitoring and direct guidance that work best to help you develop the skill and stick with it. Some expert guidance at the outset, especially with the first three, will allow you to learn the skill and discern the benefits more fully.

Meditation. There are many forms of meditation. The approach I recommend is *awareness meditation.* During each session, you practice observing, or witnessing, without judgment or purpose, whatever is on your mind or in your body, and you let it go. This weakens the normal grip any matter may have on you. It is a method of developing *mindfulness.* In the present context, practicing meditation can free you from the grip of any one pressure and foster a more complete inner awareness of your key values. It also facilitates the process of discovering creative resolutions to competing pressures.

Self-hypnosis. Similar to meditation, self-hypnosis can be an effective way to disengage from the pressures demanding your energy. You learn to go inside your imagination to a special place. It is like taking a mini-vacation. Once you learn how to do it, you can do it almost anywhere you have privacy. Because you are letting go of the usual pressures that dominate your mind, including conscious analytical thinking, your inner mind can more readily bring creativity to the concerns that are vying for your attention.

Yoga. As with meditation and self-hypnosis, there are many different forms of yoga. In the present context, I recommend using yoga to serve as a disciplined physical, mental, and spiritual practice that focuses your attention inwardly and fosters inner alignment, calm, and a sense of well-being.

Nature Walks. Taking a walk outdoors amidst the natural elements like plants, birds, and "real" weather is one of the easiest and most beneficial things you can do to restore your good energy.[71] It does not require training, money, or special equipment. When you get outside, you naturally become more in tune with the rhythms of nature. Without effort, the rhythms of your mind and body will start to shift to a more natural state. You experience a loosening of the grip of pressures of your normal life, can shift into a reflective thinking mode, and thereby discover insights for managing pressures.

Prayer. Some executives use prayer and reading of scripture as a core part of their strategy for maintaining an inner balance. Both can help put life into a larger context and connect you to religious beliefs and rituals that can be centering and comforting.

Massage. Available in a number of different forms, massage can be useful to restore inner alignment, a sense of well-being, and energy, in addition to getting relief from the physical tension that can accumulate in our bodies.

Interpersonal Processing. Let's start with the obvious reality that once you add another person to how you manage your pressures, it necessarily becomes more complex. We all know that coordinating matters with another person will go best when it is handled with mutual respect and consideration and in the spirit of cooperation. Yet the reality is that achieving that can be challenging. The interactions can easily become contentious as each participant strives to get what he or she desires.

My aim now is to point out some factors that have a large influence on how it goes. (Specific guidelines are presented in chapter 12.)

The attitude and mind-set you bring to the table will have a great effect on all that transpires. One of the more powerful ways you can improve the interactions is by making certain you both are *genuinely* aligned with a shared mission: to achieve a workable agreement that is considerate and respectful of each other *and* of the relationship. You should expect you will each be required to contribute to this and anticipate that it is anything but a steady state. As in the movie *The Defiant Ones*, there will be power struggles at times. Nevertheless, as you acquire a history of successes in resolving the battles, the emergence of the battle can serve as a reminder to realign yourselves. Sometimes that requires calling a "time out" so you can center yourselves and get realigned with the overriding mission. The better you get at managing the process in this way, the less time you can spend embroiled in the battles and more time seeking viable solutions.

It is the norm that high-level business executives find it more challenging to coordinate pressures with their life partner than with their subordinates at work. There are three key factors that deserve special attention. One is the obvious difference in role that is required in your personal life where you are ideally a co-CEO of your household and family life but may feel you are second in command. A second is that there are more personal and emotional dimensions that must be considered. The third is the likely difference in familiarity with family and household issues. These are so important that you and your partner will have to actively work on staying aligned in ways that are viable for both.

At its best, this strategy calls for you and your life partner to seek more than the proverbial win-win outcome. When done well, you each feel free *and* supported to follow the agreed-upon course of action.[72] The crème de la crème is when you each are devoted to the other doing well—a wonderful component of Synergy for Success.

For that to happen, you will each need a deeper appreciation for what matters to the other. I recommend that you make the term *conversation* a part of the vocabulary you use with your partner because it promotes the elements of respectful mutual reflecting on the matters, which can buffer the natural tendency to get into power struggles.

These conversations, of course, will go better when you are personally centered. Neglecting to do so is an invitation to get into a struggle with your partner. Take your personal processing as far as you can on your own, which may include consulting with someone else. Then show up prepared, being sure to acknowledge any unresolved aspects for which you would like assistance.

Creating regular times, structures, and routines for your conversations will take some experimenting. One useful model is to a schedule a weekly thirty-minute session with each of you getting half. You can alternate who goes first each week. Each person uses their fifteen minutes to review progress in managing pressures and identifying concerns. If one of you cannot show up at the designated time, it is important that you support the routine by requesting that the time gets rescheduled. Likewise, if more time is needed, that should be requested.

There are several advantages to having this kind of structure.

(1) The time is set up so you know you have it. It becomes a normal part of what you do, like reviewing your agenda each day.
(2) The expectation of having the regular conversation will prompt you to reflect in advance on which issues you need to coordinate with your partner.
(3) It makes it more likely that you will discover any competing issues because your partner brings them to your attention.

Casual conversations are useful as well, sometimes essential, but they do require a modicum of structure to minimize misunderstandings. You must be sure that you both have the time, are in the frame of mind to have the conversation, that you are explicit about its importance, and what you expect of the other.

My wife and I have found it useful to do a few simple things that make for clearer and cleaner interchanges (and fewer hard feelings!). After all, despite our wishes, there are times or days when one of us is just too busy, preoccupied, or tired to pay good attention. So we start by doing a status check:

"Are you in a place where you can listen to me talk about X?"

"I need to talk with you about Y. Is it okay to bring it up now?"

"I just want to share what happened today with Z. Can you listen?"

We've learned it is better to be honest if you are the one being asked to listen. How do you do this without hurting the requestor's feelings? It takes some practice.

"Well, I need to leave in five minutes" (or "Right now, I'm really exhausted") "so can you give me the short version now? Then if we need to, I have some time first thing in the morning, so maybe we can pick up again then."

"Gee, I'm really sorry, I am just not in a place where I can get into that with you now. It sounds important, so let's be sure to make some time to talk while we are driving to the meeting on Friday."

With practice, thoughtfulness, and sincerity, you will find that these interchanges are effective a majority of the time. That's not to say that when a request is declined by the other person you won't feel disappointed. You can learn, though, not to take it personally. If you respect the other person when they find it necessary to decline your request and avoid attempts to guilt them into responding, then the relationship emerges unscathed. It is your responsibility, of course, to let the other person know if you need to talk about something that is truly pressing.

Taking Action

The remainder of the book provides detailed guidelines for taking leveraged actions that can reduce energy drain, increase energy recovery, and support your efforts to stay cool in the executive hot seat.

·-·

Make It Happen

Step One. Set up your PPS. Choose the visual representation that you will use to map out the areas of your life that you want to monitor, and create it now. If you prefer, you can follow the guidelines for completing the self-administered checklists. Step one establishes an initial baseline measure and sets up a system to increase your awareness of how you are doing at later points.

Put the time in now, and you will see admirable ROIs!

Step Two. Initiate the process of setting up your conversations with one buddy and yourself. Be sure to set up designated times and a preliminary format.

Step Three. Select the pausing method you will use for mind-body alignment and formulate the initial guidelines for when you will do it.

Chapter 5

REGULATING YOUR OPERATING SYSTEM

Our minds can easily become like very expensive cars
with great engines and accelerators, but poor sets of brakes.

—W. Timothy Gallwey

Do you remember the relief when going out for recess in grade school? Can you recall the anticipation of spring break and summer vacation? Have you noticed how most performance-oriented settings build in a break, such as halftime in a football game or intermission during performances of the arts?

We often take breaks for granted, though we usually look forward to them. The exception, as noted in the previous chapter, is the tendency for ambitious people to get stuck in not taking breaks during the workday. The aim of this chapter is to supplement your respect for the value of breaks (described in chapter 4) as one basic way to optimize your performance, with seeing how simple and effective they can be.

In fact, much of the control you have been looking for in stress management methods can be found at the basic level of regulating your mind-body operating system. The strategic use of controlled pauses in the workday will enable you to regulate your energy. Then you can:

○ perform at your best,
○ deal with more pressure while experiencing less distress,
○ minimize the risk of inconvenient breakdowns.

In order for you to regulate your mind-body system while it is in action, you need monitoring methods that function as an advanced warning system: spotting the signs that the stress *reaction* is happening soon enough so you can take *constructive* action. When your methods are sufficiently sensitive and timely, you gain the option of *deciding* how and when to *respond*. A closer look will aid your understanding.

Self-Regulation 101

When you drive, you continually *monitor* the gauges, traffic and road conditions, street signals and signs, and location in relation to destination. Each bit of data provides information that you can use to regulate your driving.

What happens if while driving you are so deeply absorbed in thinking about the meeting at your destination that you fail to notice the changes in the driving conditions? Perhaps the temperature has fallen and now the road is icing up. The longer you take to recognize the traction is deteriorating, the more at risk you become. The sooner you recognize the changes, the more options you have for altering the way you are driving in order to reach your destination in the best way.

So it is with monitoring the messages from your mind-body operating system. However, it is nice to know that there are simple and reliable methods to offset your tendency to focus so much on where you are going that you neglect the status of your mind-body system. With practice, you can achieve the same proficiency with your mind-body system as you have with driving your vehicle.

Learning to Self-Monitor

Self-monitoring in the moment provides the information you need to self-regulate while in action. Mindfulness, introduced in the description of meditation in the previous chapter, serves as the foundation for self-monitoring. When you master the skill of fluidly shifting back and forth from being absorbed in what you are doing to being an observer of your own mind and body, you can make the adjustments you need to bring your best abilities online. As you become aware of the external situation, as well as of your private experience—your thoughts, emotions, and physical sensations—you can regulate how to respond outwardly to what is happening.

Mindfulness is not really a new skill to learn. It is something you do everyday, so all you have to do is learn to do it more deliberately. For example, take what happens when you are in a social situation and become aware of an itch in a private area. It is your awareness of the itch, and the situation, and your judgment that it would be inappropriate to scratch yourself, that enables you to resist the urge to scratch! Similarly, mindfulness can provide you with the essential awareness needed to choose how and when to respond to any pressure, for example, your need for a break or nourishment, or to your increasing frustration with a task or client.

Improving the Skill. It is easy to train yourself to be more mindful of the elementary components of your system. Even though the intense engagement of work tends to pull your attention away from self-monitoring, it is possible to make mindfulness a ready response. Though it may be awkward at first, with practice, it will become effortless, fluid and always slightly in the background of your conscious awareness.

Here's how to start. Do this simple exercise, the four-step monitor (see figure 5.1), once each hour, a minimum of five times a day, during work, and at least a three times a day, including weekends, while not at work.

Four Step Monitor:

Once each hour pause; notice/observe/witness

1. a breath—simply follow one breath
2. activity of the mind—be aware of what is on your mind
3. sensations in your body
4. what you are feeling emotionally

Figure 5.1

This exercise is particularly useful to train yourself to approach any absorbing activity mindfully. The goal of the exercise is for you to develop the habit of self-monitoring just like learning the habits of monitoring your vehicle's side and rear view mirrors. Do it for two weeks and observe what happens. Use deliberate practice. Some people find it helps to keep a journal of their observations to reinforce the learning. Remember, you are in training. Instead of expecting big changes, be sure to appreciate the JNDs (the just-noticeable differences) in self-awareness. At times, you will be pleasantly surprised, perhaps a bit disconcerted, as you become more aware of your body sensations, thoughts, and emotional reactions.

When you want to take your capacity to be mindful to the next level, then practice meditation. Each time you meditate, you are developing the capacity to step back and observe yourself, to be aware of your thoughts, emotions, and physical sensation, without judgment. Because this reduces the usual self-consciousness and discomfort with self-awareness, you become more aware and thereby better able to self-regulate.

Receiving the Stress Messenger's Signals

At the most basic level, your monitoring system should be receiving the *take-a-break signals* (see figure 5.2) from the stress messenger. They are telling you that you (your mind-body system) are becoming distressed and need to rest in order to recover your energy.

Take-a-Break Signals

- feeling a need to stretch, move about, or take a break
- yawning or sighing
- finding yourself hesitating and procrastinating, unable to continue work
- noticing your body getting tense, tight, and fatigued
- pangs of hunger
- awareness of a need to urinate
- feeling "spaced out"; your concentration is poorer; your mind wanders
- slight memory problems
- making careless errors

Adapted from Rossi 1991

Figure 5.2

Managing the Stress Reaction

When you get the stress messages you must heed them so you can regain control of your mind-body in an efficient and effective way. There are three main levels of intervention methods.

Level I—Brief Timeout

Give yourself a break. Call a timeout! Any kind of break that fully engages your attention, so that your focus shifts away from whatever is provoking you, will generally bring about at least a reduction in the intensity of the distress.[73] Some executives take a short walk; some read a nonwork article or make a brief social telephone call. Think of this is a much-needed chance to just "catch your breath."

Level II—Release

There are instances when the distress continues to reverberate and you need to reduce it further in order to deal with the matter at hand. At such times, you can do the equivalent of a soft reboot on a computer to *purge* your mind-body entanglement. Use the following methods alone or in combination for this purpose to:

- do some physical activity to discharge the stress hormones,
- vent your frustrations,
- use a relaxation method to calm your body down.

Physical activity, especially vigorous exercise, allows the body to release the stress hormones. Essentially, you are releasing the energy that the body has mobilized to deal with the stressor. Though physical activity alone does not change what has been bothering you, often it is accompanied by a spontaneous flow of emotions and thoughts that lead to better perspective when you resume your efforts to deal with the issues.

Venting emotions has a similar effect by discharging the emotional energy that has gotten triggered. Once it is purged, it is easier to revisit the troublesome matters and to work with them in a more constructive way. Guidelines for releasing emotional energy are presented in chapter 7.

Relaxation methods enable you to interrupt the automatic reaction of the sympathetic nervous system (the part that mobilizes resources for the fight/ flight reaction); and activate the parasympathetic nervous system (which evokes the relaxation response that calms the body).

Mental Reactivity
(Worry, Fear, and Fretting)

Relaxation
Response

Physiological Reactivity
(Rapid heartbeat, tension, sweating)

As depicted above, during distress the mind and body feed off of each other—this is the *autonomic stress response*. Worrisome thoughts trigger body activity such as rapid heart rate, breathing, and muscle tension, which your mind interprets as cause for concern, exacerbating the worries. When you become aware of either the mental or physiological reactivity, you need to *interrupt* the automatic cycle by inducing the opposite of the stress response, namely, the *relaxation response*.[74] Then you can resume dealing with whatever triggered the reaction with a clearer mind and calmer body.

When you induce the relaxation response, you get a reduction in distress and a sense of relief, even more than what you gain from a simple break. So, to reboot your system you can use one of the relaxation methods described below. They are efficient and effective, and they enhance your control of your basic operating system.

While there are more refined ways to invoke the relaxation response (e.g., progressive muscle relaxation, and meditation, self-hypnosis, and yoga as described in the previous chapter), start with the two simple methods below that are based on controlled breathing. It is crucial that you become convinced that these methods work so they become permanent residents in your operating system.

It is crucial that you become convinced that these methods work to get them "installed" in your operating system. A good way to discover the merits of any of these techniques is to do a self-rating before you start it and then another afterward. On a scale of one to ten, with ten being extreme distress, give yourself a rating of how tense, anxious, and distressed you are. Just take a mental note of what you observe. For most people even a small shift to a lower rating is enough to validate the method is having the desired effect.

Be sure to observe any changes in your mind and body when you resume your normal activity. Though you may feel slightly subdued as you first shift back to work mode, within moments you will feel refreshed and able to bring better energy to whatever you need to do.

4-8-8 Breathing. This relaxation method (see figure 5.3) is simple, fast, and effective and can be used in almost any situation. Practice the exercise with your eyes open, so you can inconspicuously use it in a wide variety of situations, even when you are with other people. Occasionally someone may notice and may say something like, "Hey, you look a little spaced out." You can always reply, "Yeah, I was just thinking about something.

As you become more experienced, you will find you become absorbed in the sensations in your body. You may feel the sensation of air coming into your nostrils, expanding your lungs and the attendant pressure, relaxing your lungs with relief, experiencing a slight fuzziness of your consciousness. It is this absorption that allows you to disengage from whatever mind-body-spiral set off the stress response. When you are first starting out, go through the steps three to five times in succession to get a more noticeable effect. Gradually, you will find that all you need to do is start the method and you will trigger the calming response. Essentially, the initial steps become a ritual that initiates a cascade of changes in your mind-body system.

4-8-8-Breathing Method

1. Breathe in slowly and deeply through your nose to the count of four at the rate of 1001, 1002 ...
2. Hold your breath to the count of eight at the same slow rate.
3. Exhale through your mouth to the count of eight (same slow rate).
4. Observe any positive changes in your body and mind.
5. Resume your activity or repeat as needed. (Because you are holding the breath, you cannot hyperventilate.)

Figure 5.3

Finger Breathing (see figure 5.4). This is useful when you are experiencing distress or any time that you want to gently disengage from pressures. It is a structured method that is easy to learn, calming and self-centering. This method helps you to focus on visual and sensory-motor sensations that serve as an anchor for your attention. In so doing, you gently coax your attention into the here-and-now; as you bring your focus to the current moment, you disengage from whatever has triggered the stress reaction.

Give yourself time for the gradual shift in absorption to occur. At first, you may notice that you are distracted by the external environment and by your own thoughts and feelings. As you continually redirect your attention back to the exercise, the other stimuli will slowly recede further into the background. It is as if you were saying to the disturbed part of yourself, "No, I am going to focus here instead of on whatever is distressing." Persist, and you will notice a subtle shift as you become more focused on your visual and bodily sensations. Continue through two or more sets of all ten fingers until the desired sense of calmness and self-centering has been set in motion.

Finger Breathing

1. Find a private and quiet spot that is free from distractions and interruptions. If your options are limited, a bathroom stall works.
2. Sit comfortably with both legs on the floor. Place the palms of your hands on your lap.
3. As you look at the little finger on one hand, slowly inhale. Imagine a string connecting your breath with the finger so that the in-breath lifts the finger and the out-breath lowers it. Raise the finger slowly so it feels as if the breath is lifting the finger. As you exhale slowly, allow the finger to descend in unison with your breath, as if it is lowering the finger.
4. Focus your attention on observing the finger as it moves, noticing the sensations in the finger and the sensations in your lungs. As you become thoroughly absorbed in what you are seeing and feeling, you will disengage from whatever was provoking you.
5. Progress to the next finger and continue through each finger on the first hand. Now move to the thumb of your other hand and breathe with each finger until you reach the little finger. Then reverse the process until you are back with the first little finger. Taking slow, deeper-than-normal breaths will allow you to become absorbed in the finger-breath connection.

Figure 5.4

Level III—Reset Yourself

Sometimes you need more than to be free of the distress—you may also need to adjust your mind-set before you resume your efforts to deal with whatever threw you out of kilter. At such times, once you have calmed your system, it is best to deliberately reset your perspective. You can do that in three ways.

Find the Trigger. Take some time to reflect on what was happening when your stress response was triggered. What was it that triggered your reaction? Can you formulate a better way to handle your challenge?

Visualize the Solution. There are times when thinking about how to manage a troubling situation can only take you so far. Furthermore, you may not have anyone available to help you sort out your situation. At these times, you may be able to get insights on how to handle the situation by doing a mental rehearsal. If you visualize yourself handling the situation well, walking yourself through each step in your imagination, you may find unexpected resources. You will find that you go back to the challenge feeling calm, composed, self-assured and ready to take action. This is a common way that athletes and actors use self-hypnosis to visualize doing all the right things, mentally and physically, prior to going into action.

Full-On Stress Reduction Method. The following nine-step stress reduction method (see figure 5.5) brings together the exercises noted above and provides a comprehensive and structured way to manage distress. Modified from a six-step stress-reduction method developed by Mort Orman,[75] it is adaptable for immediate, short-, and long-term distress. As you gain experience with it, you will remember to use it sooner in the process and will get results faster.

Nine-Step Stress Reduction Method

Step 1. Develop mindfulness.
Step 2. Recognize your mind-body signals.
Step 3. Use a self-regulation method.
Step 4. Identify the *specific* problem.
Step 5. Relate to your problems as "feedback."
Step 6. Identify the specific thoughts and behaviors that are causing the stress response.
Step 7. Remind yourself: these hidden causes exist in your body, not your mind.
Step 8. Take action to neutralize these internal causes.
   Stress Dissipates!
Step 9. If your distress doesn't disappear, repeat steps one through eight and/or get coaching.

Figure 5.5

1. **Be mindful**. Learning to monitor your moment-to-moment experience without judgment leads to awareness of fluctuations in the activity of your mind and body.

2. **Read your own signals.** With mindfulness, you can identify the mental and physical activity that alerts you that your stress response has been triggered.

3. **Take charge.** Reduce the momentary distress by using a level I or II interrupt method. Repeat until your mind and body are calm enough for you to regain at least a moderate level of composure.

4. **Identify the *specific* problem**. It is essential that you discover the specific problem that is troubling you. Instead of focusing on a vague sense of feeling tense, stressed, or overwhelmed, ask yourself what specifically is bothering you. For example, "The phone keeps ringing and interrupting my focus, the deadline for this paper is tomorrow, and I have to take my child to band practice tonight!"

5. **Consider your distress as feedback.** Make the assumption that the root of the stress response resides within you: in the meaning that the trigger has for you, or something that you are doing or not doing that contributes to the automatic response. Then, when you observe your stress response (the tension in your body or the mental anguish) you need to shift your mind-set to, "The stress messenger is trying to tell me something about this situation. I wonder what that is!" Ask yourself, "What is the distress telling me about what is going on *within* me?"

6. **Identify the *specific* thoughts and behaviors causing trouble**. Adapt a mind-set of curiosity (to bypass your natural tendency to be logical) so you can *wonder:* "What is it about the way I am thinking or what I am saying to myself about this stressor that is causing me to feel distressed?" "What is it about the way I am handling this problem that is causing the distress?"

> You will find it helpful to label your internal comments and self-statements as a *private conversation*. Doing so will give you a bit of distance, so you can step out of the grip of these automatic thoughts. Some common examples of private conversations that lead to frustration include

"I am not succeeding."

"I should be able to succeed easily in this situation."

"If I don't do this successfully today, it's because I am stupid, dumb, weak or incompetent."

Similarly, you will get better results when you label the way you are going about trying to deal with the stressor as an *action pattern*. Examples include:

- attempting to meet unrealistic goals and expectations
- holding yourself to a rigid, inaccurate definition of "success"
- failing to relate to your "failures" as "feedback
- trying to work alone rather than admitting that you may not know how to succeed or you might need help from others

7. **Remind yourself: "I can change my automatic thoughts and behaviors."** Your private conversations and action patterns are embedded in your "core operating system." They neither define you, nor do they arise from rational thinking. As such, these ways of thinking, perceiving, and acting are automatic patterns that were taught to you, often through the modeling of significant people, especially family members.

8. **Neutralize your enemies.** You can take control of your automatic reactions and shift to more constructive and realistic responses to the pressure you are facing.

Replace stress-producing conversations with realistic, positive self-talk. Initially you might say to yourself, "I am not succeeding at closing the deal on this contract. I should have had this done last week! I just don't have what it takes! " Neutralizing this inner conversation would allow you to put the problem in perspective and take the specific situation into account. You might start by recognizing that you are distorting the truth. When you look at the situation more objectively, you might realize that there are some special aspects of this contract that require unique resolutions. As you acknowledge that you are breaking new ground, you may also realize that you actually have made progress in several important areas.

Break stressful patterns. Are you stuck in a pattern of behavior that repeatedly gets you into trouble? Perhaps you frequently try to do too much with too little time, cramming four hours of work into one. When you can recognize the absurdity of your goal, you can revise your plan and create a more constructive course of action.

Create stress-relieving options. Whatever the source of distress, you can alter the context so that you open up opportunities for resolution. One general, potentially very liberating, change is to seek assistance. Successful people are quick to realize when they need help and are good at enlisting the best resources.

Stress Disappears!

9. **Repeat steps one through eight (or get coaching help), if necessary.** If the distress persists, you may find that going back through the steps helps you to discover another crucial element. If your efforts do not yield appreciable results in a timely manner, seek a buddy, mentor or coach to assist you.

Using the nine-step stress reduction method can alert you to the sources of distress that tend to crop up repeatedly. You will find that you develop an internal checklist of triggers that serves as a sort of shortcut when you seek to identify what has set you off in any specific situation.

⌐⌐⌐⌐⌐⌐⌐⌐⌐⌐⌐⌐⌐⌐⌐⌐⌐⌐⌐⌐⌐

Make it Happen

Step One. Try out each of the two level II simple relaxation methods (4-8-8 Breathing, and Finger-Breathing). Notice how you feel before and right after doing each exercise: changes in your mind (amount and type of mental activity) and body (sensations in your chest, shoulders, face). Then make another observation in about ten minutes. Choose the one that you will practice regularly (three to four times each workday for two weeks). That is sufficient for you to become more aware of how your mind and body are when calm, and to foster the habit of using the self-regulation methods. This greater awareness of being calm will also sensitize you to when you are becoming tense.

Step Two. Try out the two level II rest breaks. Aim for at least three rest breaks in the course of one workweek. Notice the differences in your feelings and thinking before and after. Note especially the differences in your body, its state of tension-calm, and your mind, the extent of confusion-clarity before you took the break. Compare that to the level of calm you feel afterward and the improvements in your thoughts about what you need to do when you resume.

Step Three. Once you have gotten comfortable with the level II exercises, you are ready to move on to level III. You may want to try the two simple reset methods first. However, it would be best to do the nine-step stress reduction method. Aim to use it once a day for two weeks. Be alert to changes in your mind and body when you finish the last step of the exercise. You will know that you have had an impact on your stress reaction when you sense a noticeable shift (one or two JNDs of reduction) in mental and/or physical activity. You might find it helpful to jot down your observations as a way to increase your awareness of the patterns you tend to get stuck in.

Chapter 6

MANAGING A PERSONAL ENERGY CRISIS

Great leaders are stewards of organizational energy.
They begin by effectively managing their own energy.

—J. Loehr and T. Schwartz

The biopsychological imperative of your mind-body operating system requires a steady supply of high quality psychological and physical energy to perform optimally. Deficiencies in your energy reserves will cause your mind-body system to operate in *distressed* mode, undermining the use of your personal and professional resources and skills. Unable to tap into your best abilities, you will not be able to capitalize on business opportunities. Further, you will be more likely to elicit nonsupportive responses from your support system because your social-emotional skills are waning. The convergence of these factors puts you at greater risk of diminished self-esteem and life energy.

Energy is simply the capacity to do work. Our most fundamental need as human beings is to spend and recover energy.
—Jim Loehr and Tony Schwartz

While it is true that some people just naturally bring good energy and inner composure to the pressures of the day, your aspiration to perform optimally as a CEO means you must manage your particular energy requirements. Doing so requires you to become attentive and responsive to the foundation of your psychological and physical needs with the aim of fostering synergy amongst the main aspects of your life. In this chapter, you will learn how to bolster your core capacity through self-care strategies that nourish your psychological and physical reserves.

The objective of this chapter is to make it easier for you to acquire the wisdom Tom Hood, CPA, executive director and CEO of MACPA, learned from the school of "hard knocks."

I have learned to listen to my body. The biggest part of this has been a journey to understand myself and how I deal with the different situations.

83

When I wasn't managing that right, I would run myself down and get sick ... dealing with that and recognizing the kind of signs of oncoming situations that might increase the stress got me to an awareness of the value of monitoring.

Now I try to anticipate those [situations]. I call it managing energy. The energy required to handle lots of different things can be immense at times, so I've learned to look for that. When I know when I'm going to need a lot of energy I make sure I'm doing the right things. That might be resting properly, eating, exercising, doing something to make sure I'm recharged.

Psychological Energy

Alignment with Core Personal Values

One primary source of good psychological energy is that which you derive from living a life guided by your core personal values, when you are, as psychologist Martin Seligman points out, authentically happy.[76] In this context, you can use your PPS to monitor how well you are adhering to your core values by regularly reviewing the Core Personal Values checklist you completed in chapter 2. Then use the Personal Asset Allocation checklist (chapter 4) to monitor how well the various aspects of your life are affecting your energy.

Another way to monitor your alignment with personal values is a pie graph that represents your life. Mark off slices of the pie to signify the main areas of your life (work, family, recreation, self-care), sizing them in accordance with your values and ideal distribution of time and energy. Identify a lower limit within each slice that represents the point at which you are about to enter deficit mode. That builds in a buffer range, similar to making sure you replenish the toilet paper supply when there is one left—not none.

You can make this a routine part of your PPS by shading in your status on each of the key areas to gauge how you are doing at attending to the most important facets of your life. Some people substitute a wheel of life image for the pie. It gives them a visual representation of how smoothly their life is rolling. (You can easily adapt these monitoring methods for use with role, personal, and social well-being to which we now turn.)

Role Well-Being

When you have positioned yourself in a role and work environment that suits you,[77] you get ongoing energy from both. (See chapter 12 for more information about the work environment.) One of the requisite underpinnings of being cool is the energy you derive from being personally aligned with your role, having a clear grasp of your obligations, and engaging the support of a loyal team. These all contribute to creating the desired synergistic impact on your energy.

Let's take a look at a few key psychological dimensions of role well-being.

- The *personal meaning* that you take from your job influences your general attitude toward your work and how you engage your role. Both of these greatly affect whether or not you will have the energy and determination needed to sustain a high level of engagement over time and changing circumstances. When your job provides intrinsic satisfaction, you gain an ongoing source of energy even during hard times. You engage its pressures and responsibilities as opportunities to move agendas forward and as challenges to master the process.

Pressures in your personal life can have a large effect on the congruence of your job and the energy you derive from it. One participant in the project left a higher-paying job in the private sector to provide important leadership and organizational development for a public institution. Upon accomplishing his goals within the organization, he became more concerned about the risks to his family's lifestyle caused by the continuing pay reduction. He realized then that the job was no longer a good fit and that he needed to return to the private sector.

- Your *competency* for doing the job can, of course, bolster or drain energy due to the effort it takes to perform your duties. It is important that you periodically evaluate the specific skills required in various areas of your job.

For example, some individuals are competent in leadership skills yet have weak organizational skills. One of the people I interviewed was convinced by his colleagues on the board of directors to take over the presidency of an institution, in large part because he had proven himself as a very successful entrepreneur. However, he had little experience with organizational management and did not know the specific industry well. Our interview took place during his first year in his role. The poor guy was anything but cool: he was in over his head and floundering in a sea of everyday demands.

Another interviewee had extensive experience prior to becoming CEO: he had been COO, CIO, and Executive VP and appeared to have all the requisite competencies. Much to his chagrin, he found the demands of being CEO to be much more challenging. His ability to be cool took a big hit, and he was expending an enormous amount of effort.

In contrast, several other CEOs rose up through the ranks and found the transition to CEO quite manageable.

However you got into your position, it is important that you take stock of your strengths and weaknesses and address them regularly. The methods in this book will help you sustain your cool in many ways, but they do not address matters such as your capacity to do the work. Any deficiencies are not only a drain on your energy but a significant source of angst, and they will undermine your capacity to be cool. Keep in mind, too, that as the business evolves so will the demands, and it is vital that you regularly take stock to identify and improve any shortcomings[78] in your skill.

> The *mind-set* you bring to your role is one of the more powerful influences on your energy reserves. It shapes how you perceive and feel about your tasks, how you strive to achieve your objectives, and the ways you manage the demands of your work. Without the proper mind-set, you are more likely to feel confused about what you should do and not do. This will cause a sense of uneasiness, and sloppiness in your management approach. Once you learn to monitor and regulate your outlook you can have a powerful

Set out to be the best you can be, but don't expect to be perfect. If you set yourself up to be the all being, all master, you are going to end up in a mental home.

—Clinton Wingrove
Project Participant

inner stabilizing force that, like a gyroscope, helps you stay mentally and emotionally centered.

The following key components of your mind-set shape the way you engage the role of CEO, its tasks and pressures. Be sure to incorporate each into your PPS so you can monitor them.

➢ Role Responsibilities

You must have a thorough comprehension of the explicit and implicit responsibilities of your role and its implications for the operation of the organization. Many executives have a natural tendency to slip into an exaggerated sense of their responsibilities. To offset this, select one different aspect of your role each month to review and reconsider your responsibilities. Additionally, whenever you feel your energy is diminished, or you are distressed, you can use that as a signal that a review and a mind-set adjustment may be necessary.[79]

➢ Attitudes and Beliefs

To bring good energy to any task, you need a strong sense of *ownership* for it. Then you will be more centered, composed, and in command. The effect is often subtle yet large. Invariably, the degree of ownership is highly influenced by the extent to which you also have a strong sense of purpose for the task. Note the difference in the following two contrasting examples.

Imagine that you are preparing a presentation for a pivotal meeting with a representative from a company with whom you hope to build an alliance. Your attitude would likely be: "This is a great opportunity! I know what I want to present, and I'm going to do what it takes to get it done well."

Now imagine your board of directors is pressuring you to prepare a presentation for them. Maybe you feel working on something else is more vital or that the issue does not require an extensive presentation, or that the timing is off. Yet to appease the board, you agree to do the work.

Most likely you would feel a large difference in the energy you have with the task in these two scenarios. Obviously, in the first one, you have taken full ownership of the work. It feels important to you, and you believe it is your responsibility. So you do it without much, if any, inner turmoil. Your resoluteness means you "just do it." Moreover, most likely you do it quickly and efficiently. You are fully engaged and in command.

When a strong sense of ownership prevails, most CEOs easily shrug off what might seem like pressure; they do not even experience it as an energy drain (distressing). "It is just the nature of the business: different things come up. It's just what I do." For those who do feel the pressure, it is often experienced as a positive: "That's the game. That's the adrenaline."

In contrast, in the second scenario, you are likely to feel put upon and irritated and may be grumbling. Your focus and work effort would be less than stellar, unless you had good reason to believe that doing the job well has a direct bearing on your job.

Personal and Social Well-Being

The energy we can derive from a secure sense of well-being in our personal and social lives, is often greater that we realize. The effects are reflected in better self-esteem, attitude toward work, ability to focus, and resilience. Too often, we only become aware of this when serious problems in our personal or social life are a drain on the energy we have at work.

Because it is to your advantage to increase your respect for this dynamic, start by making a few observations. Pay attention on two different days in one week to how your mood and energy change in response to events in your personal and social life. For example, an enjoyable recreational outing on the weekend can boost our energy and send us back to work on Monday with renewed enthusiasm. On the other hand, an argument with an important person in our lives can color the rest of the day, leaving us preoccupied and lacking in energy. To assure you give the attention your personal and social needs deserve, add them to your PPS and include a weekly review with your buddy.

Physical Energy

Nutrition. The eating guidelines in the popular press tend to focus on food to manage weight and health. There is another way to approach nutrition, which is to optimize your performance capacity. It goes back to your demands as an athlete,[80] albeit a white-collared one.

Seeing Food as Fuel. Food provides the very fuel for your physical energy. Depending on what, when, and how much you eat, food can enhance or undermine your ability to sustain good energy throughout the work day. While this seems obvious, it is a frequently overlooked factor.

I remember being surprised many years ago when I discovered how big a role food played in the ebb and flow of my daily energy. For a long time I had been aware that within an hour after eating, a wave of tiredness overcame me. It felt as though someone had pulled the plug on my energy source. I attributed this to the natural dip in energy we all have in the afternoon, which I just had to push through. A consultation with a nutritionist revealed an additional source of the deep energy drop was the high-glycemic loading of the bagel I ate for lunch. I tried switching from my beloved bagel to whole grain bread with my lunch. Not only did I eliminate the dramatic early afternoon drop-off in energy, but my energy remained more even and long lasting well into the evening.

Getting off the High-Glycemic Roller Coaster. Foods with a high-glycemic load (e.g., refined grains, like those in bagels, many breads, muffins, sugary cereals, as well as orange juice) produce a rapid surge in blood glucose and insulin. Within a few hours, those levels are suddenly reduced leading to a drop in energy and often to a craving for more carbohydrates. In contrast, foods low in glycemia (whole grains, proteins, and some fruits, such as pears and apples) provide a slow-release energy source. Nutritionists and exercise physiologists are clear that healthy carbohydrates, especially whole-grain foods, should be a mainstay of a diet for sustaining good energy.

Grazing through the Workday. The quantity and timing of your "refueling" also have a significant impact on energy levels. The Tour de France provides a good example of this since it takes the need for sustained energy to such an extreme. The scientific recommendations for these super athletes are clear: they must eat nutritionally dense foods in small quantities frequently.[81]

Most executives have sedentary jobs, so it is easy to downplay the impact of nutrition. However, to perform optimally as a white-collar athlete, you must sustain a steady, high level of energy during the entire day.[82] That means frequently eating small quantities of nutritionally dense foos.

Adopting the CEO Diet. Even when taught these well-established guidelines that underscore the importance of approaching nutrition as fuel for performance, it can be hard to make the changes. I have found that the younger and less experienced the executive, the more likely they are to be ruled by their sense of overwhelm rather than taking control. I hear, "I don't have time to think about what and when I eat," "I eat on the fly," or "Often, I get so absorbed in my work that I forget to eat!"

> *I try to eat sensibly in the middle of the day because it just helps me if I'm going to have a long day. I try not to overeat then because I find that that slows me down.*
>
> —George Bodenheimer
> Project Participant

Sometimes it is not until the person feels more established and secure in their accomplishments that they adopt healthier eating habits. Likely because these more experienced executives are less anxiety-driven, they become more aware of their daily fluctuations in energy and they feel that they can devote more attention to themselves. Increases in attention to diet also happen when executives find they lack sufficient energy to meet new challenges.

> *I'm a big believer in nutrition. So I know how not only to pace my day, I know how to pace my [eating].*
>
> —Emory Mulling
> Project Participant

Perhaps you can be smarter sooner by adopting better strategies now! Make good nutrition a key part of your efforts to master your ability to manage your personal side as well as you manage your work, so you can create a lifestyle that helps you sustain the ideal executive performance state.

Sleep. "Early to bed, early to rise, makes a man healthy, wealthy, and wise." Trite? Of course. Nevertheless, there is truth in the old adage. Here again, despite the knowledge that good sleep is vital to sustained good performance, many executives (especially those who are less experienced) undervalue sleep. Some even treat it as an unwanted intruder, often wishing they could skip it or just plug themselves into a quick-charging device. Many are sleep deprived, with the pressures to be productive interfering with what should be the sacred space of sleep.

In fact, it was my awareness of the magnitude of the problems of sleep deprivation in executives that became one of the driving factors behind the launching of the CEO Stress Project. I wondered, "How do the most successful executives let go of all their responsibilities and pressures so they can manage to sleep at night?" Drawing upon what I learned in these interviews and from the clinical research, it is clear there are some very specific ways to set yourself up for good sleep.

The ABCs of ZZZs[83]

A. *Prioritize.* The single best thing you can do to get good quality sleep is to make it an absolute priority. The ideal attitude is, "There is nothing more important tonight than that I get good restorative sleep." You may find it helpful to remind yourself that the nighttime is not a time to work. "I need my sleep so I can work well during the day."

B. *Prepare.* At the start of the day, and interspersed throughout the day, pause and ask yourself, "What must I do during the day to make sure that tonight I can let go of the day and drift off peacefully into a deep restful sleep?"

You may be able to get insights from a time when you successfully prepared for a weekend or longer vacation, when everything was in good order so you could leave with peace of mind. What did you do that made it possible for that to happen? (There are guidelines for letting go of the day later in this chapter.)

C. *Depressurize.* Do not expect to go to sleep with your inbox empty. In fact, if you are an entrepreneur or corporate executive, is your inbox ever going to be empty? As you become more successful, the projects that occupy you increase in number and importance. So to get perspective and to start identifying what would work for you to depressurize, try wondering how CEOs are able to sleep at night. The answer is not to reduce the pressures. Rather, something has to happen within you to be at peace when it is time to go to sleep. What is that?

> *The art of resting the mind and the power of dismissing from it all care and worry is probably one of the secrets of our great men.*
>
> —Captain J. A. Hatfield

Any pressure that lacks a specific plan of action is a good bet for messing with you at night. Sometimes the worries do not emerge until you get into bed, or later, after you have been asleep. If this happens frequently, the best strategy is to schedule time—before getting into bed—to sit quietly and become aware of any concerns. Then resolve that you will address them on a specific day at a designated time. Developing a decisive action plan—prior to going to sleep—will enable you to contain the concern.

It is notable that some high-level executives are so good at compartmentalizing that they rarely experience insomnia. For many others, insomnia is like the proverbial canary in the coal mine: it is a warning signal that they have too many unresolved concerns.

D. *Surrender.* There are many elements of business that cannot be controlled. Accepting this and increasing your capacity to tolerate uncertainty is a must to be able to surrender to sleep. If you are having trouble doing so, you would be smart to evaluate what improvements are needed to increase your faith in the process of your business, including the systems you have created and the relationships you have built. You will also benefit from the detailed guidelines for managing uncertainty in chapter 13.

E. *Manage.* The objective is to sleep efficiently—the time you spend in bed should be very close to the time you are actually sleeping. Studies show that caffeine can take as much as ten hours to be out of your system. Your sensitivity will generally increase with age. Minimize exercise, smoking, alcohol, and heavy meals within two hours before sleep. As a caveat, dependence on sleep medication can lead to several hazards and complex problems, although these are beyond the scope of this book.

To control the stimuli in your sleep environment, eliminate nonsleep activities (except sex), including TV and reading. Make an agreement with your partner that all conversations of substance should end ninety minutes before retiring to sleep. Increase calming stimuli in your bedroom by turning down bright lights as you get closer to sleep time. Create sleep rituals that trigger the natural shift into sleep. Going to sleep early and awakening early—at the same time each day—is best.

There will be times, even though you have done all the best things to enhance your nighttime relaxation, when something disturbs your sleep. As several of the project participants mentioned, sometimes you just have to weather the storm by letting your system metabolize whatever is going on. If these are more than occasional events, however, you should take stock to see what may be missing from your normal daytime methods of reviewing matters.

When you do experience difficulty sleeping, it often helps to get up and write down your concerns. Here's how Pamela Pine, PhD, MPH, founder and CEO of the organization Stop the Silence: Stop Child Sexual Abuse[84], described her approach.

> I'll have a conversation with myself, and it's usually a pretty short conversation: Okay, let's see, what's going on? What are you worried about? I'll sometimes get up, write it down on a piece of paper so I know that I'm not going to forget what it is that I'm concerned about by the morning. Then I go back to bed and just say, "Well, I can handle it. I know I can get it done." And I remind myself that I just need to stop. And that's pretty much the conversation.

When you are in one of those places where, as one CEO noted, "Something is just really nuts," here is another approach.

> I have to come up with a plan for fixing it. If I can't get that done right that night, then it helps to try to put it in perspective. I do this by asking, "What's the worst that could happen?" I take myself through the exercise of getting my rational mind to acknowledge that I do have to let it go because I cannot control it.

Power Tactic—Total Shutdown Routine

Learning how to shut down your system for rest is an important component of energy management, so here are some guidelines to help you do that.

Set aside a few minutes to prepare for your shut down sequence. It is best to do it about an hour before you want to turn in for the night. Reflect on any lingering concerns from the day and about resuming tomorrow. Do whatever it takes to make sure you will deal with them tomorrow. For example, you might set up a reminder in your electronic device. Then, identify and interrupt any remaining troublesome thought patterns. Label them as unessential for now while reaffirming the importance of letting them go so you can shift into calming mode. Anxious thoughts about being able to sleep should be replaced by calming thoughts and images of sleeping like a baby or pet dog or cat.

Learn one or more relaxation techniques (see chapter 5). First, practice them during the day. This enhances skill development and keeps it separate from any sleep concerns. Once you have gotten the hang of it, use the relaxation method at night after completing the mental shutting down routine (and if you awaken any time prior to your set wake up time). Be sure to tell yourself that you are doing it in order to let go of the day, to embrace sleep, and to prepare yourself to work well tomorrow. It also helps to remind yourself that tomorrow is another day and that right now there is nothing more important than restoring your energy through sleep.

Exercise. How is learning to pack a parachute correctly for a skydiver like regular exercise for a high-level executive? When I raise that question at stress-management workshops, I get some interesting replies. More often, I hear, "I don't have the time or inclination to do either!"

If I don't exercise for a couple of days, I start to feel edgy. I can just feel it ratcheting up.

—Tom Beerntsen
Project Participant

So how are they alike? In both cases, you are investing your effort in something on the front end so you can count on it when you need it the most.

A widely recognized benefit of physical exercise is its role in discharging the stress hormones that mental and emotional stress activate. Exercise cleanses the physiological system so it can be ready for the next stressful event. A lesser well-known benefit, noted by sports psychologist and performance expert James Loehr,[85]

Exercise is just a gigantic release. I think about people that don't do that. What are they doing with all the stuff that's building up? It has got to take a toll!

—Mike Skarr
Project Participant

is that it can *increase* your capacity to be hardy in response to the stress of everyday life. Stress, regardless of its source, is a demand for the expenditure of energy. A well-conditioned body is hardy, enabling you to mobilize your energy to meet pressures as challenges, and to settle back down quickly so you can recover for the next challenge. On the other hand, a weak body is less resilient than a well-conditioned one. As one CEO put it, "The pace you have to go with these jobs, you need to be physically fit."

Ron Peltier, MBA, CEO of Home Services of America, Inc., and chief real estate strategist for Warren Buffett's Berkshire Hathaway team noted, "I need to be in the right place to deal with high-stress cycles. That means I need to make certain I get exercise. Regardless of what is happening, I've got to be in control of my own physical being. I can definitely feel when I get more exercise; I've got an inner calm which seems to take over."

Getting Started. Exercising is a lot like dieting. You can go on a diet, but studies show the best approach is to cultivate healthy eating habits that you will follow over the course of your lifetime. Likewise, the best way to approach exercise is to think of it as a lifestyle modification. When you know you are going to be doing it for the rest of your life, you are more likely to approach it in a way that emphasizes satisfaction. (It might be helpful to review the guidelines for change presented in chapter 3.) Making a commitment to the long-range plan is crucial. Without it, you will never *find* the time to exercise. You must elevate exercise to a level-one priority, right up there with good nutrition, rest, and satisfying personal relationships. Then you will *make* the time for it.

Loehr's research shows that to build hardiness for managing daily stress, your program should incorporate more than one type of exercise, including aerobic, stretching, and weight training. You also need to vary the intensity level within each workout since stress in daily life does not happen at the same pace throughout the day.

Making Time. The challenge of making time to integrate exercise into one's daily routine can lead CEOs to leave it off the schedule despite knowing its value. "I can't find time in the day. I start real early in the morning and I try to find time for my devotional time and my quiet time and a quick shower. And by that time, everybody's starting to wake up and I'm being Dad and I'm driving kids to school, and the work day starts right then and it doesn't end until I'm picking kids up from swim practice at 6:15 p.m."

Sometimes, the challenge is more emotional. "If I am facing something where a very large effort is going to be required of me and I don't have a great degree of passion for it, I will tend to make compromises that are really not good for me. I'll say, you know I've got that big meeting tomorrow, it's going to last all day; I don't want to work out today."

While there is no one solution for integrating exercise into your daily routine, it will only happen when you make it a priority. The executives who sustain a regular exercise routine generally do so by putting designated workout times in their schedules. That way, it is not a daily decision or a question. They just do it! Furthermore, they are protective of the time. Those who are committed to exercise, in fact, tend to handle unavoidable disruptions in their workout regimen by rescheduling the missed workout whenever feasible.

Some prefer working out first thing in the morning and others after work. Some executives have a home workout area with exercise equipment that allows them to use their time more efficiently. One CEO walks regularly every evening and swims each morning unless he has an early meeting. Another found that he needed to make exercising a component of his workday to make it happen reliably. He scheduled his daily workout as part of his business schedule. To add to his incentive, he hired a trainer who charges whether or not he shows up.

ˑˑˑˑˑˑˑˑˑˑˑˑˑˑˑˑˑˑˑˑˑ

Make It Happen

Step One—Do a Status Check. You need some data to make these guidelines more meaningful. Review the evaluation you did in chapter 2 using the Personal Asset Allocation Worksheet. Then do a quick rating again at least two times over the course of one week. Complete your ratings at the end of the workday on Monday and Friday to see if/how your ratings change over the course of the week.

Research has shown that relying on memory is too impressionistic to give valid results. The self-report measures give you real data that you can use to establish your starting baseline. As you integrate more of the components recommended throughout the book, you will be able to compare their effects.

Want additional convincing data? Get feedback from a trusted coworker and a friend or family member. Have them rate you on the Personal Asset Allocation Worksheet and provide any general observations they can. Be sure to convey your sincere interest in getting candid remarks. Let them know you are doing this to improve your overall work performance and satisfaction in your personal life.

Step Two—Identify Desired Improvements. Now think about how improving your energy management will enhance your performance and fulfillment. Are you looking toward improvements in general attitude, mental sharpness, or perhaps emotional resilience throughout the day? Are you driven by the prospect of improving your capacity to maintain composure during especially frustrating meetings? Or to work well on challenging tasks such as preparing a presentation to the board of directors? Are you thinking about how better management of your energy during the workday better would bring you home in better spirits? Identify the changes that are most important to you.

Step Three—Formulate Initial Goals. Formulate specific, measurable, and time limited goals regarding your personal self-care. Be sure to make the goals specific enough that you will know if you accomplished them or not. Keep your goals modest yet meaningful. It is important that you succeed and that the improvements really matter to you. The key element in fostering mastery is that you become convinced of the value of what you do, so you feel invested in sustaining it and interested in developing more refinements.

Chapter 7

MAKING EVERY DAY GREAT

To be fully engaged, we must be physically energized, emotionally connected, mentally focused, and spiritually aligned with a purpose beyond our immediate self-interest.

—J. Loehr and T. Schwartz

Wouldn't it be nice to arrive home at the end of your workday feeling genuinely good about how you managed the day's pressures and your own energy, satisfied with the quality of your productivity? There is a deep sense of well-being that comes from knowing that you honestly did your best—that your mind and body were filled with vigor and you were fully engaged as you met the challenges of the day.

In the final analysis, it is this sense of well-being that allows you to feel pleased and proud of yourself, as well as to forgive yourself for any disappointments. In addition, the sense of satisfaction about your work performance, and how you managed your energy during the day, contribute to having good energy for your personal time. It also contributes to good sleep, thereby setting in motion a synergistic effect that carries through to the next day at work.

Well, you can make this happen once you know how to set your sails for the day's trip!

In chapter 6 we reviewed some of the major lifestyle factors that affect overall energy, including nutrition, exercise, and sleep. In this chapter, we turn to managing your energy over the course of a day.

Engaging the Day the Hardiness Way

The mind-set you bring to the day makes a large difference in your energy for the day's activities and how you handle your tasks. The following graphic provides a concrete example of how perspective operates. What do you see? A young woman or an old woman? How you see "her," of course, has a direct impact on how you relate to her.

Do you naturally engage the new day in a way that leads to optimal energy? In keeping with the Hardiness for Hard Times approach, you want to be sure your mind is set in the best way for the day, and this is something you can intentionally cultivate. The following methods are quite effective. None of them require a full-scale pep rally.

You can start by taking a couple of lessons from the way successful CEOs align their attitude for their work. These high-functioning folks take full *ownership* for their day. Even if they sometimes briefly grapple with getting mobilized first thing in the morning, they quickly shift into take-charge mode. They rarely bemoan their work because they focus on their *career*. They engage the pressures and responsibilities as opportunities to move agendas forward and to improve their skills. One CEO noted that he enjoys his work so much that the line between work and nonwork frequently is blurred. In fact, many CEOs feel their work is a calling. In this way, it often takes little conscious effort for them to engage their workday.

On the lighter side, Clinton Wingrove, the CEO and principal consultant of Pilat HR Solutions, provided the following glimpse into his morning mind-set.

> I come into the morning knowing that if the day is going to be typical, there are going to be things that I am going to enjoy, things that are stunningly boring, and things that are difficult and, therefore, could be stressful.
>
> So I wake in the morning planning that the day is going to be enjoyable. No matter what I am doing, there is always a side to it that actually can be enjoyable—I am learning something,

interacting with someone else, clearing the deck, or focusing on doing something more efficiently or more quickly.

Imagine what your workdays would be like if you combined that mind-set with that of a company president who engaged each day determined to achieve maximum output with minimal distress! Even though we often assume that these attitudes are operating, that is not enough. The real power lies in embracing it—when you intentionally set them as the *overriding values of how you engage the day.*

Ask Yourself These Questions

The following questions will help you do a status check on your current mind-set and consider how you might improve your approach to the day.

- Do you deliberately think about what would constitute a good day, an enjoyable day, or a productive day as you get started in the morning?
- Do you have a clear sense of how you will know at the end of the day if you met your objectives?
- Have you reflected on how your mind-set influences your feelings when you leave work and shift into your personal life? Consider the attitude you bring to your family when you arrive home, as well as other personal indicators such as how well you sleep at night.

I assure you that each day you take charge of your mind-set in these ways you will be rewarded. Changes in some areas may be only one JND (just-noticeable difference) better, but the extent of changes in other areas may surprise you.

Prime Your Mind-set to Engage the Day

Successful CEOs know they have to hit the ground running. So they develop routines—like a pre-game strategy and pep-talk meeting—to get intellectually and emotionally prepared.

Power Tactic—Hardiness for Hard Times Ritual

One simple yet potent way to mobilize yourself for a great day is to use a ritual that mobilizes the Hardiness for Hard Times mind-set. The value of a ritual is that it automatically has the desired effect with minimal effort or self-discipline.

Start with a morning review of your plan for the day. Now, wonder how someone who is hardy would approach this day. You might want to imagine a particular person who epitomizes the qualities you most want to have. When you engage your imagination, a technique often used in self-hypnosis, you set your mind on a search for the ways that will work for you.

Suppose your schedule includes

(1) Completing a report that is required by the board of directors. You generally think of this task as a waste of your time, yet only you can do it and it is due tomorrow.
(2) Conducting a dreaded meeting. You dread this one because you expect that it will be emotionally demanding.
(3) Meeting with three of your favorite executives. This will be a meeting to brainstorm a new initiative, an activity you enjoy and are good at.

The "hardiness" mind-set makes it more likely that you will find ways to manage the pressures so they are

(1) congruent with your needs

 ➢ Do the report first so you use your best mental energy early in the day to get it out of the way. Or plan to do it at the end of the day so you don't squander your good energy on it, and make sure the time you spend on it doesn't fill too much of the day.

(2) transformed from dreaded pressures into challenges

 ➢ Your goal for completing the report may be to formulate the essence of what is needed to do the task well enough; complete it in an amount of time that is pushing the realistic time needed; reject any internal complaints that arise by asserting, "Just do it!"

> ➤ Your goal for managing the meeting might be to practice your ability to stay composed; empathize with staff concerns; genuinely respond to staff concerns in a way that recognizes them as an important part of the organization's needs.

Power Tactic—Morning Ritual

Anytime you find that priming your mind-set for the day is particularly challenging, try modifying the ritual described above so it is more structured.

Here is an outline of the steps for a morning ritual. Modify it as needed to suit your situation.

1. Create a quiet special place where you can be alone and undisturbed. Get composed by first using a relaxation exercise, meditating, doing a few yoga stretches, or by listening to some calming or inspiring music.
2. Review your long-term goals, your deeper and more compelling values, and mission related to your image of success and the good life.
3. Review your current personal and professional growth goals. What qualities are you trying to improve in yourself? (Character? Coping? Interpersonal, management, and/or leadership skills?)
4. Do a frank appraisal of your status with personal and professional goals in comparison to where you want to be in the next ninety days.
5. Mobilize your determination to bring your best energies to the day by identifying why it matters for you to put forth the effort.
6. Plan your day, designating times for specific tasks including time to reenergize yourself. Identify the three most important things you must accomplish today, and be sure to give them a slot in your schedule.
7. Reaffirm your determination to improve any recurrent weaknesses.
8. Visualize how you want your day to go, targeting any special meetings, encounters, and work sessions. Imagine potential trouble spots and see yourself responding with the qualities that are most important to you in the situation (e.g., precision, composure, poise, self-assurance, creativity, friendliness, and optimism).

9. Imagine yourself at the end of the day feeling very proud of yourself for how you dealt with the day. What will you see, feel, and think? Identify three private victories that you will achieve during the course of the day.

You might find it helpful to tell your life partner or buddy a summary of your plan and make an agreement to review how it went at the end of the day. The more structured routine should mobilize your determination to engage the day as a series of *challenges* and that you feel ready and eager to do whatever it takes to meet the demands. The outcome is that you feel physically energized, mentally focused, and in control. Then you can also expect feelings of distress and dread to diminish markedly, perhaps dissipating entirely.

Staying Energized All Day

Some CEOs are not aware of energy fluctuations during the workday, so they feel no need for renewal. Camouflaged by intense involvement, these executives tend not to notice the warning lights on their own dashboards. Then there are those who deliberately soldier on because they have the misguided notion that the only way to sustain energy throughout the day is to keep going.

It doesn't even occur to me think about taking a break. It is not even an option to consider letting my guard down. I just keep going. At the end of the day I am totally exhausted.

—Project Participant

These patterns persist despite the biopsychological imperative of managing energy for optimal functioning. Remember, the *major challenge of being a CEO* is to integrate self-management with your focus on work. To achieve that you must make energy management a high-level priority. Then you can set about developing the habits that improve awareness of your mind-body signals and efficient ways to regulate your energy.

A smart way to approach these improvements is to remember that you are training yourself. It will take deliberate effort and practice. The goal is that you will have a new set of automatic behaviors that work effectively and with minimal struggle. Because self-awareness plays such a crucial role, a good place to start is to use the following questions to identify what you already know about the signals you get about the status of your energy.

> How do you know when you are mentally performing well? Poorly?
> What are the physical sensations that tell you your energy is good? Poor? Waning?
> How can you tell when your emotions are enhancing or detracting from your work?
> How do you know when you are fatigued from expending too much energy?
> What are the signals that let you know you are sleep deprived?
> How do you know when you need food? Water?
> What happens when you are feeling overwhelmed?
> How do you know when you are not being challenged enough?
> What other signs and signals alert you to fluctuations in your mental, emotional, physical, and spiritual energy?

Just by paying more attention to these signals, you will also become more aware of some meaningful patterns. It can be as simple as noticing what happens when you ignore the signals that you are hungry for too long. There is a point when you are likely to find it difficult to concentrate, you become impatient, and have difficulty regaining your equilibrium even after eating.

Improving Self-Monitoring

It may help to realize that you are retraining yourself to self-monitor—it is the natural way of children. The challenge is to refine your ability to know what to be aware of and what to do with your observations so you can accomplish that with ease. It is like what you do when you are driving a vehicle.

The first step is to build the habit of monitoring your energy. Start by adding several specific times to your PPS routines when you will do status checks. Three times, spread out over the course of the workday, for two weeks should be sufficient. Use the four-step monitor method described in chapter 5 that is designed for this. Remember, the purpose is to help you automatically become more sensitive to your patterns.

Processing

Being more self-aware does not automatically result in improved energy regulation, any more than does noticing that you are running low on fuel in your car. It is just information. However, with that information you gain the option of deciding what adjustments to make and when to minimize big performance swings due to lack of adequate energy. Consider the following.

> ➤ How do you know what kind of renewal you need?
> ➤ What are the options for recovering energy?
> ➤ What are the benefits of meeting the need?
> ➤ What are the risks of overriding the need?

The Art of the Fresh Start

Even small breaks in the day can refresh your mental energy in the same way that stretching refreshes your body. You may decide to take a walk to the water fountain or have a brief social chat. In these quick breaks, your mind-set is very task focused: you are taking a break so that you can return to work shortly with better energy. You do not dawdle.

Not all workplaces support the need for breaks. One of the more absurd ways this shows up is in offices where employees are not allowed to take breaks, *unless* they *need* to have a cigarette! Of course, in many offices, employees sneak a break by surfing the Internet, an activity that surely wastes more time than a walk to the water cooler!

For some people, the idea of taking a break is so foreign as to be initially perplexing. "I know I need to take breaks, but I'm not sure what I would do with myself. One thing I wouldn't mind doing, that I have thought about and think would help, is to take a walk, or do something constructive like that. Just get a clear head."

There are other executives who have learned to make the brief break a regular ritual. One respected executive even goes out of her way to stop in a colleague's office to hassle him, just to get an energy shift and boost. Others have a little snack or take a short walk around the building or the block.

Sometimes a more extended break is needed, such as when you need to recover more energy after a strenuous meeting or need a power boost in the middle of the day. Social contact does this for some people, and they may dedicate some time to visiting with a colleague or calling a friend to chat. Others seek solitude, closing the office door for some quiet alone time, which may include reflective thinking, listening to music, or reading something unrelated to work. A walk outside or even around the office building provides a good disengagement from pressures. You will get the best benefit from a break if you label it as a needed time out.

Ed Kelley, CPA, CFE, CFO, Boys and Girls Clubs of Annapolis, not only realized the value of breaks but found a way to leverage his time away as an incentive for meeting his work goals.

> I used to get to work at 7:00 a.m. and work until 6:00 p.m. or later. I ate lunch at my desk. I found that to be very ineffective. I was there. I was busy. But productivity was not good. So, I insisted that I have a lunch break.

> Now, I eat at a conference table, go to an empty office, or go out. I focus on that as a reward for meeting the goals of the first four to six hours of the day. I say, "If I get this done, then instead of just going across the street to the supermarket to get a sandwich, I'm going to go to a sandwich shop and eat in." That gives me a reward of eating, as well as a reward of relaxation.

When efficiency and effectiveness are paramount, a good way to recover and focus your energy is to use a relaxation method in combination with rethinking your goals for the remainder of the day. That's where the "power break ritual" comes in.

Power Tactic—Power Break Ritual

Many people find that the structure of a well-defined relaxation and refocusing method is the most efficient and effective way to recover their high-level functioning. Determined to perform at their very best throughout the day, they place a high priority on making their breaks count. That is the driving force behind the Power Break Ritual—a systematic way to recover maximum energy with minimal effort or disruption to daily routines. You can create a true mental and physical break from the normal pressures of the day, recovering energy and mobilizing yourself to accomplish specific outcomes. It is an empowering routine because it draws on a deep sense of purpose that provides a mental guardrail to focus your efforts.

When you incorporate the Power Break Ritual into your day, you will find that the ROI will more than make up for the time you spend. By enabling you to work better when you resume work, you gain more effective and creative thinking, reduce distress, and build greater resiliency in dealing with interpersonal pressures. Think of the Power Break Ritual as being like what a football or basketball team does during a crucial game when the coach calls a time out. In the time out, the players get a full break from the intensity of the game; they may consume an energy drink, while they plan their strategy for how to reengage the game.

Make the power break a ritual during your workday by repeating it over time so that it becomes automatic. Gradually, you may find that looking forward to it helps the work that precedes it go better.

The essential ingredients are to:

Disengage. The objective is to temporarily free yourself from all demands for energy output so your mind-body system can naturally recover. Just like when you exert yourself physically, white collar athletes need to stop their activity to recover energy. Ideally, the break should last for twenty minutes.[86] By using a relaxation method, you get the greatest benefit from your effort as compared to less systematic ways. Examples are meditation, self-hypnosis, yoga, and tai chi.

Refuel. Take five minutes for a healthy nutritious snack to provide the fuel your system needs to perform well for the remainder of the day. The best foods to maintain a steady energy flow are low glycemic foods such as almonds, apples, cottage cheese, some nutritional shakes or bars, pears, pumpkin seeds, or organic yogurts. Be sure you only eat as much as you need (100-150 calories) to sustain your energy for the remainder of the workday, and drink water to rehydrate your system and to aid in digestion.

Reengage. When you disengage, you may briefly feel as though your energy has been depleted, and you may not want to engage anyone or anything. This happens because you have released the stress hormones. While it can be disconcerting at first, you will find that you get used to it and learn to trust the process. Once you start back to work, your good energy will return (usually within five minutes).

Since this is a power break, take a few minutes to set your specific goals for the remainder of the day to assure that you reengage with optimal energy quickly. Make sure they are attainable and meaningful. Answer the following key questions with specific detail:

- What time am I going to leave work today?
- What do I want my evening to be like?
- What do I need to do with the remaining time at work to feel pleased and proud of what I accomplished?
- What is my strategy to make that happen?

General Guidelines. Feeling a little skeptical that a power break ritual can work for you? A common first reaction to the idea of using it is, "I don't have time for this!" A trial period will likely convince you of the ROI. It is reasonable to expect that when you resume work you will be more effective and creative, less distressed, and more resilient in dealing with interpersonal pressures. Do it once a day for two weeks so you can become convinced of its effectiveness, and you will look forward to it each day!

Letting Go of the Day

· · ·

There's a law of diminishing returns: the incremental value of staying that extra hour to answer two more emails has limited incremental value to what you do at work, but has significant incremental detrimental value to your at-home life.

—Thomas Modly
Project Participant

· · ·

One of the greatest challenges you face is letting go of work at the end of the workday. Doing so is what allows you to start the next day invigorated and ready to work optimally. For that to happen, your mind-body system must be completely free from the mental and physical pressures at the end of the day so it can fully recharge.

People who are hardy see this as yet another challenge that needs to be mastered. So, they develop strategies for letting go. Fortunately, you can too.

Transitioning from Work to Home

Successful CEOs accomplish letting go by two complementary methods. First, they *compartmentalize* their workday, separating it from the evening. At the end of the workday, they put business matters into a mental box. Then the evening becomes its own box—a time to *not work*—and they let go of work concerns.

The second step is that they engage in regular *routines that help them to shift* gears into a nonwork mode. With clear intent to unwind and flush out the day, most have routines such as having a relaxed dinner with their life partner and immersing themselves in a hobby or reading nonwork books before retiring to sleep.

Power Tactic—Letting-Go Rituals

When you need a more compelling strategy, start with a review of times when you have succeeded. What worked? Then refine it with practice so it becomes a ritual. There is no "right" way to accomplish this. All that matters is that it has same effect as if you have turned off one switch and turned on another.

One CEO does a mental check at the end of the workday to determine if he did his best. He asks himself, "Did I give everything I had in what I was supposed to do today? Did I work on the big things?" He has discovered that he finds release in the certainty he has worked well enough on the most important matters to let the smaller items go until the next day. He noted that this has to include an honest assessment of any remaining matters. By doing this at the end of the day, he also primes himself to handle the next day even better. Two CEOs described environmental cues that helped them to shift gears from the work world to their personal life. One had to cross a long bridge on the way home, and she knew that by the time she got to the other side she was in the world of her family. Another executive always entered his house through the front door when he arrived home from work. Not only was he entering his home life through that door, but as he closed it he was shutting the door on his work life.

An interesting twist on the letting-go part of the day was offered by a young company head who stated that he relishes having some unfinished big matters at the end of the day, because then he can be excited about tackling them the next day.

Make it Happen

Step One. Consider your morning routine. Do you have a ritual for starting the day that brings focus and determination to your mindset? If not, how can you improve the start of your day? Write a brief but detailed description of your new and improved morning routine. Tomorrow is the day to start it.

Step Two. Review the self-monitoring guidelines in this chapter to see what you need to target for improvement. If you discover any aspects that are not identified in the chapter, but that you know are valuable to you, be sure to note them. How do you monitor your energy status over the course of the day? Make a list of the signs that your energy is waning and consider how you might benefit over the course of the day from deliberate attention to your internal gauges. Add some notes about how you will respond to your cues in order to maintain a more consistent store of energy.

Step Three. Select one of the three rituals described in this chapter and plan how you will incorporate it into your workday. Do it every workday for a week. Be sure to use the guidelines for deliberate practice described earlier in the book to assure that you derive the best value from your efforts.

Remember, whatever you select and do, your aim is to make a difference in some way that matters to you. The goal of the trial is for you to discover the differences you can affect by practicing your chosen ritual. It is your belief in the value of your efforts that will fuel your determination to continue with the behaviors and for them to become cherished rituals in your day.

Chapter 8

THE MYTH OF MULTITASKING

It is only when we are giving our full attention to what we are doing
that we can bring all of our resources to bear effectively.

—W. T. Gallwey

In your eagerness to accomplish as much as you can within limited time, you are at risk of mistaking high volume of activity for meaningful productivity. In this chapter, you will learn just a bit about how brains work so you can adjust your manner of working to the type of task you are working on. Some simple strategies will help you set up your work time to fit the reality of the working brain. Then you can be more productive while maintaining your cool.

Multitasking—or Not

Have you ever heard someone boast about how well they can multitask? Sounds good, doesn't it? In fact, this is an illusion. Advances in brain-imaging technology prove the human brain is not capable of multitasking.[87] What actually happens is that the brain is shifting from one task to another at high speed, performing rapid serial processing. While we may have the perception that we are multitasking, we are really juggling tasks.

For some people, this so-called multitasking brings a delightful sense of power and control because they have the illusion of handling so much at once. Not surprisingly, though, they may easily slip into feelings of overwhelm, because efficiency and effectiveness in dealing with each task is diminished by this switching activity. Furthermore, there is mounting evidence[88] that the more time we spend with rapidly changing stimuli, the more we experience erosion of the ability to stick with tasks that require focus and concentration.

For tasks that require only small bursts of attention and effort, juggling them may be fine. For example, it may be effective for rapid replies to electronic messages and phone calls. However, it is not effective for complex tasks that require more focused attention and deeper concentration, such as preparing documents or planning and organizing your work.

Focus Is Formidable

For tasks that require focus and concentration, a different work style is needed. To be fully engaged and immersed in a task requires you to set aside other tasks. For some, this is hard to do. A common problem is that executives experience conflict between their various responsibilities. On one hand they feel obligated to be at meetings and easily accessible to their staff. On the other hand, they need time to work on their own projects and to plan. Too often this conflict makes it difficult to "justify" the need to step out of the action and the flow of information in order to work.

Even when you do step away, you may need to find ways to settle your mind for focused work. After the often hectic pace and interactive nature of your tasks, the shift may not be automatic, as Pete Stark, chief information and security officer for the US Postal Service, pointed out.

> I know I need to consolidate meetings and telecoms more in order to free up space for myself. It's funny. You get so hyped up when you have consecutive meetings that when you get back to your desk and find you have some "free" time, it is difficult to get your mind around it and to think that it is okay to have it. You really have to reset your mind to take advantage of it.

When you coach yourself to take advantage of your sacred work time, you set the stage for your most productive efforts. The purposeful mind-set—"Now I am going to focus on this piece of work"—feels satisfying because you are taking control. The same result happens when you make explicit what you will *not* to focus on.

Ron Peltier also finds it helpful to coach his staff to focus, particularly during high-stress times when they are especially vulnerable to distractions. He reminds them, "Stay really intensely committed to what you're doing right now. Don't let your mind wander, and don't be thinking about what you're going to be doing."

Power Tactic—Brain Guards

For those situations when you must fully immerse yourself on a task, you must be able to protect yourself from the intrusions that are so often a part of the everyday work environment. Like guardrails on the highway, you need "brain guards" to protect your mind from distractions.

You can start building your brain guards by considering the following: What can you do to protect your mental and physical space from disruptions? How can you take control of what is streaming into your brain?

This is nothing new. Surely, there have been times when you were able to create uninterrupted work time. For example, many businesspeople point to the hours immediately preceding an important presentation as a time of intense and effective focus. What specifically did *you do* that made that level of focus happen?

Your reflections are most likely to reveal the following key factors:

✓ You had a clear sense of purpose combined with well-defined goals and deadlines.
✓ You felt a mandate to take charge of all distractions in order to achieve your objective.
✓ You took specific actions to shield yourself from intrusions and distractions.

Working Smarter

In the final analysis, you want to work the best ways you can. Brain guards require strong intention and specific, highly focused actions to be effective.[89] It is a real challenge to create the boundaries needed to block disruptions while preserving necessary and sufficient accessibility to the people and information that help you to manage the other facets of your responsibilities. It is also a challenge to direct your internal energy as you shift to the focused work required for many aspects of your job as a high-level executive. However, it is this ability to adjust your external and internal boundaries that allows you to work smarter. Using the strategies laid out in this chapter, you will find you gain in your feelings of control and your productivity.

Make It Happen

Step One. Draw from prior experiences to start getting back in control.

- Identify three times in the past when you were successful in creating and maintaining a viably focused work zone for concentrated work.
- Select the one that epitomizes what you need in order to purposefully put your brain guards into place.
- What specifically did you do that enabled you to have that success?
- Consider how you can apply that to your present situation.

Step Two. Identify any competing agendas you have that get in the way of focusing. Perhaps there are some subtle signs that can that can help you here. Do you find yourself seeking distracters even when you have the opportunity for quiet, solitary work? Is there some uneasiness that you need to address to align your behavior with your intentions? Identifying your own mind traps will help you to stick with your plan.

Step Three. Consider the following questions in order to work smarter. When you seek to answer these questions, you activate your inner search engine. Your mind will continue to ponder the information and significant ideas will emerge, like pop-up windows that offer additional information. Put the information to good use as you set up your brain guards. Dedicating even a small amount of time (as little as ten minutes) to developing systems and processes for working smarter can have long-term benefits.

- ➤ Is the amount of time you have designated each day for specific tasks adequate?
- ➤ Which tasks are you spending too much time on? Which ones can you delegate? Which ones require complete focus?
- ➤ How can you improve your strategies for managing specific short-term deadlines, intermediate goals, and long-term projects?

➤ How often and what do you need to review to stay aligned with your goals?

➤ Who can you consult with to sharpen your planning?

➤ Who can you consult with to help you set up and monitor your use of brain guards?

Chapter 9

RENEWING YOURSELF

Inside myself is a place where I live all alone,
and that's where you renew your springs that never dry up.

—Pearl S. Buck

No matter how well you use the present methods to stay cool, you cannot immunize yourself from the gradual buildup of strain caused by being "on" so much—including "being plugged in and ready" even when not fully activated. There will still be a level of strain and depletion that can build insidiously. Since you cannot fully avoid this dynamic, it is essential that you learn how to manage it.

Managing starts with understanding, so we turn now to a brief review of how the various parts of an individual may struggle with the CEO part that can be a relentless taskmaster. Just as you read about the need for brief breaks throughout the day to maintain your best energy on a daily basis (see chapter 7), renewal from career stress over time also requires breaks, but on a larger scale. Your career feeds the parts of you that are tied to being a CEO. To the extent that you disregard other parts of your identity and personal needs you unwittingly create deficits. Unchecked, you will experience gradual erosion of your whole being. There comes a point when other facets of yourself demand that you attend to them, without regard for the timing or impact on your intended agendas.

Sometimes the way that deficiencies in self-renewal announce themselves is in the form of waning energy and depression. Other times, the announcement comes in the form of impulsiveness—the loss of self-control leading to the overuse of alcohol, food, drugs, or sex. Or perhaps it shows up as spending mindless hours watching TV and roaming the Internet, indulging in excessive sleep, or overfocusing on acquisitiveness. These are unimaginative, sometimes desperate ways of trying to feel free on the cheap. The dynamic is one of *stealing* freedom rather than psychologically liberating

· · ·
All work and no play
makes Jack a dull boy!
· · ·

oneself. The result? Lack of replenishment, further erosion of good energy, and the ever more compulsive repetition of the self-indulgent behavior. The outcome is a crash of some sort, often in the form of burnout, when the person cannot go on—the "soul has departed."[90]

It is in this context that self-renewal gives meaning to the notion of maintaining a balanced life. Similar to the value of a nutritionally balanced diet, there is essential value in meeting the minimum requirements of your needs as a whole person. Moreover, one participant noted that it takes more effort to reverse a downward spiral than it does to maintain a steady or upward spiral of energy. This is the flip side of the Synergy for Success model, both of which argue for being more attentive to your other-than-CEO-parts on an ongoing basis.

Stop Fearing Freedom

Despite all the good arguments for integrating self-renewal into your routines, there are mental traps that can interfere with fully embracing it. Let's look at three of the most common.

The first and deepest one is that while people like to think they want to feel free, as Erich Fromm explains in his classic book *Escape from Freedom,*[91] real freedom scares people. Freedom *from* restrictions and control can result in feeling isolated, anxious, and powerless. As a result, many people seek involvements to give themselves a sense of security. They create intense work involvements that they then experience as *demanding* their time and effort.

In fact, anxiety over being free can underlie the most admirable behaviors, such as the tendency to be overly generous, conscientious, hardworking, or devoted. Because others benefit from the wonderful qualities and deeds of such individuals, even loved ones can fail to realize when the behaviors are excessive and come at great personal cost. Recently a local business owner, a man who was very successful in creating a popular business and who was revered for his generosity to the community, committed suicide. When I read about his suicide, I thought, *Now there's a man who could not take care of his personal needs!*

The second mental trap that can interfere with embracing self-renewal is the occupational hazard of being so enmeshed in your career that you do not maintain awareness of, or perhaps even truly understand, your other needs well enough to be *able* to satisfy them. Left unmanaged, this can lead you into a deeper hole, making it even more difficult to get out. The prudent strategy is to reserve some minimum amount of time each week to make room for other interests to emerge.

The third trap is that avoiding down time can be a way of avoiding the complexity that arises from self-awareness. The pushy part of your personality, that feels compelled to produce and that chastises you when you are not being "productive," likely overshadows your thinking about your work agenda as well as your personal goals. When you pause, you are more likely to question your plan. For example, you may notice that your agenda is unrealistic. Of course, while your reflections in the pause may allow doubts to surface, ultimately this puts you in a better position to take control and to modify your expectations. In so doing, you will be better able to maintain a more effective and sustainable level of ongoing effort.

"Sharpen the Saw"

Once you grasp that the need for renewal is a *need*, not a luxury, then you can set about finding the best ways to achieve it.

You can embrace self-renewal and genuinely appease your ambitious side by framing what you are doing as *accomplishing* the recovery of good energy, what Stephen Covey referred to as "sharpening the saw." It might help, for example, to remind yourself that you are relaxing or doing some nonwork activity *because* you want to be ready to engage your work the next day with your best energy. Because there is no prescription or one-size-fits-all method for renewing yourself, you will need to do some exploring. Then you can evaluate the effectiveness of your renewal efforts by assessing the level of physical-psychological-emotional-spiritual vigor you bring back to your work.

If you have a life partner, you may have some negotiating to do in order to feel free to do what you need to for yourself. For example, you may find that achieving a sense of freedom depends on having the flexibility of agreeing that you and your life partner can go your separate ways for a day or two. During this time, you do your own thing with the comfort that comes from knowing your relationship is secure. As long as what you do is liberating *and* maintains the integrity and trust of the relationship, go for it!

Whether you choose to spend the time alone or prefer to spend it with your partner, the choice of what you do in your renewal time is limitless. You may delight in artistic expression, religious practice, volunteer work with a community group, hanging out with friends, taking a cooking class, going for a stroll in the woods, tending to your garden, gazing at the flames in a fireplace, getting lost in a good book, or relaxing in a hammock while listening to the birds and insects sing.

Becoming Whole

Self-renewal comes from two seemingly opposing processes. You restore your depleted pool of energy by *engaging* in activities that allow you to express and experience the other-than-CEO parts of you. Often there is no purpose in the activity except your enjoyment of it. You also renew yourself by *disengaging* from all the involvements in your life. Let's consider each of these processes, in turn.

The Engaged Self

Aside from your work, what do you love to do? What activities do you eagerly move *toward?* You know you them by feeling fully free of pressure and regimentation. You feel drawn into the activity, with little effort required to stay engaged. When this happens, it is like meeting again a friend that you have betrayed.[92]

Not everyone can readily come up with a list of compelling activities. If this is new for you, begin with what you already know about yourself, the types of activities and involvements that mean a lot to you. Who are you in addition to being a CEO? What are the other parts of you that need to be fulfilled? When have you felt the most pleasant, at ease, at peace, joyful, gratified? What else in life have you derived satisfaction from? What have you longed to do that you have been putting off until a different phase of life? Maybe you have a bucket list.

Be sure to include the other roles you occupy such as spouse, parent, or religious schoolteacher. Add to your list the activities you sometimes enjoy, such as hobbies, sports, reading, artistic expression, cooking, entertaining, or participating with community, political, or religious groups. There may also be activities that are difficult to categorize but that you enjoy, such as spring cleaning or going to yard sales. What is important here is that you pay attention to any activity that feels so satisfying that it feels as though you are scratching an itch when you are involved.

Many CEOs are drawn to reading and are pulled into a good mystery or crime story or drama. For some, reading is a ritual that enables them to compartmentalize—they shift gears as they pick up a book or start up their e-reader. Reading literature also helps to get different perspectives on life and can be a source of inspiration. While some CEOs read very light "word candy" to get relief from the strain of the day, others find devotional reading helpful.

When you have a hobby, it is like having a good friend you can easily turn to without obligation. There is no pressure. It is all about doing what feels enjoyable. A hobby can be wonderfully absorbing in an easy and satisfying way that offers payback of a very different sort than does your career.

Several CEOs I interviewed emphasized the personal benefit they derive from community service. For example, Al Verrecchia, the CEO at Hasbro, Inc., is on the board of directors for a local children's hospital. His visits with hospitalized children during the Christmas season serve as a powerful reminder to put his life in a better perspective.

Admittedly, some people are uncomfortable with their various interests because they do not "fit" with their own image of a business executive. I have heard CEOs sheepishly acknowledge their interests in participating in Civil War reenactments or watercolor painting. Yet psychologists believe that mature adulthood happens when you embrace the various facets of yourself and blend them into a complex sense of who you are.

Still searching for your own interests? This is one of those PPS *conversations* you need to have with yourself, as well as, perhaps, your life partner or buddy.

The Disengaged Self

Another aspect of renewal flows from the process of *disengagement*. You nourish yourself at a deeper level when you are *detached* from the usual activities of your life. When you experience yourself as a completely separate entity from all the roles, responsibilities, attachments, and involvements that ordinarily "define" you, you nourish your soul.

There are different ways that this disengagement can occur. It can happen naturally when you are involved in a nondemanding but absorbing activity, such as music, prayer, yoga, or meditation. A slow walk outdoors can help you to disengage, or you can allow yourself to be entranced by a sunset or the fire in your fireplace.

Sometimes, detachment occurs when you make a *decision to let go* of everything. You may have had the letting go experience when you are a few days into a two-week vacation, when you pause long enough to feel your exhaustion and finally surrender to the need for a nap. The experience mirrors your mental state when you are first drifting off to sleep or when you lie back on a float in a pool and allow your mind to drift.

These are instances of what psychologists call naturalistic trance or hypnotic states, characterized by a feeling of floating in the space between here and there. Sometimes they are called a meditative state. During the experience, you are free of pressure and judgment, and you are at peace with yourself. It is YOU just being in the moment, hovering, feeling safe, secure, carefree and spontaneous. You gain an even deeper sense of well-being when you give yourself this experience as a *choice* you make. It is an expression of genuine caring for yourself, rather than a *command*. It is you being in control of your own revitalization process.

As you consider ways to build renewal into your life, I want to add a brief note about the research on television and renewal. Watching television is often used to disengage from the pressures of life, though it is gets stiff competition from surfing the Internet. These activities should be used judiciously at best. Too often, watching TV is used as a passive escape, a distraction. While that does have its place, research[93] shows there is a downside that makes it incongruent with your goal of functioning optimally. Specifically, television is highly stimulating so you do not relax in ways that restore your energy; may foster values that run counter to the ones you are intending to have as the main drivers of your life; *captures* attention and often leaves people regretting how much time they watched TV; and does not provide healthy solutions to the problem of internal "noise."

So how do you currently detach yourself? How often do you set aside time for you own renewal? Remember, self-renewal is a need, not a luxury.

Make It Happen

If you are a person with a clear path to self-renewal, one who already has nonwork passions and ways of disengaging with the outside world, then go directly to step three.

If you are at a loss for activities that might bring the revitalization that you need, start with step one.

Step One. In order to discover (or reawaken) the activities that feed your soul, you must start a query process. The best way to do this is to set a context for the gentle, mindful internal search. Create an undisturbed place to disengage with the outside world by following the guidelines that are recapped here. Remember, this can be a real place, such as a special spot in your house or yard or perhaps it will be a quiet refuge where you can take a stroll. It can also be a place in your imagination that you take yourself to while meditating, such as your favorite beach or a beloved hiking trail out in the woods. All that matters is that you are able to experience a total and complete feeling of safety and comfort, with no pressures and no demands. All bad jokes aside, some people think of this as their "happy place," others as their safe place.

Now, just let your mind wander with no intention except to remember experiences that have engaged you in such a pleasurable way that they became memorable. You might wonder about times that you have felt passionately and fully absorbed in an activity. Where and when has that happened for you?

Step Two. Identify three to five activities that you have been able to lose yourself in at some time in your life. Consider how you can bring one or more of these activities into your life with minimal disruption to your daily/weekly routines.

Step Three. Make a commitment to engage in the desired activity by designating the time on your calendar. What would it take for you to arrange a one hour respite once a week? Be specific regarding other people; any responsibilities you have; any internal prohibitions (thoughts, feeling, values, beliefs) you have about relinquishing an active, responsible, "doing" way of being; and any other matters that might interfere with your capacity to psychologically let go. Set that appointment with yourself as a sacred opportunity for the renewal that brings vitality to your daily life.

Chapter 10

EXECUTIVE COOL

The first lesson is to remain calm, not to panic.
Because emotions are called "hot cognitions,"
this is known as "being cool."

—Laurence Gonzales

People like Michael Jordan and Chuck Yeager epitomize being cool—remaining calm, composed, powerfully focused, and in command in the face of intense pressure. At crucial moments they were able to do just the right thing.

Perhaps you will never face life-or-death challenges like Chuck Yeager did as a test pilot, or the intense pressure to make a perfect assist with two seconds left in a championship game as Michael Jordan did as a basketball player. But you will certainly face situations in your business dealings every day where "being cool" can make a decisive difference in the outcome—situations when you must handle a pivotal interaction with a staff member or customer, make a key decision, or make long-term business plans in the face of uncertainty.

In his book *Deep Survival: Who Lives, Who Dies, and Why*, Laurence Gonzales[94] notes that the contemporary use of the expression "being cool" originated with the African American jazz musicians in the 1940s. Refusing to succumb to getting "hot" in the face of the racism that often emerged while they were performing on stage, they learned to channel their fear and anger into focusing on the matter at hand—playing their music.

Now imagine how much better your work experience and your performance will be when you have trusted ways so that you can stay cool. You not only can, but you must!

To start, you need a clear sense of what you are striving for. I propose using executive cool to refer to the *ideal executive performance state*. It refers to the complex inner workings that function like a gyroscope, global positioning system and autopilot do on a ship. While

You've got to be able to juggle some balls and not get too emotional.
—Project Participant

· · ·

navigating through the seas with variable wind force and water currents, these systems maintain the ship's stability and hold to the course. With these basic functions well handled, the pilot focuses on monitoring the systems and making adjustments as needed along the way

As a CEO, you must be able to keep a cool head in the *many* situations you face, and you've got to be able to reliably do this over the long haul. Executive cool means you are seaworthy. You have the composure and capacity to keep your wits about you and to function optimally under pressure. You are mentally, emotionally, and physically unwavering so you can effectively manage the whole deal of what it means to be a CEO.

One person who had been CEO of several corporations advised, "If you're really going to make it in a corporate world, you can't be getting too upset about things all the time ... your fellow cronies expect you to perform and be ready, and to be emotionally stable."

Don't think you have the exceptional natural ability to stay cool like Chuck or Michael? Few people do, but surprisingly few people realize the extent to which this capacity can be developed. Keep in mind that both of these cool performers had a lot of focused training and did huge amounts of deliberate practicing.

The underpinnings of your capacity to be cool include the many self-management and self-care practices described in the preceding chapters as well as the supportive work environment and relationships that are addressed in chapter 12.

This chapter provides guidelines for developing two dimensions of being cool even as you respond to the heated conditions of the moment:

> **Behaving Cool**—the cognitive and behavioral methods for staying composed and in control of yourself at the moment when you are faced with an intense challenge
> **Appearing Cool**—presenting the appearance of being cool to protect your image in order to best serve your staff and the public

Behaving Cool

Thinking on Your Feet

Key to your facility to be cool when faced with provocative events is your capacity to use reflective engagement—especially in the moment when you are facing a high-pressured situation, like Michael Jordan preparing to take that last shot. In the business world, this takes the form of situations like needing to deal with a provocative interaction with someone or being on the hot seat to make a pivotal administrative decision. This is what people refer to as being able to think on your feet, or having your wits about you. It is a powerful self-management skill that enables you to regulate the interplay of reasoning, emotions, physical needs, and behavior in response to the immediate situation.

It requires a kind of mental gymnastics.

> You shift and flow from being involved in what is happening to figuratively stepping back so you are disengaged enough to observe the process to:

  ○ reflect on what is happening
  ○ formulate a best response to it
  ○ prepare yourself mentally and physically to make the desired response
  ○ shift back to the interactive engagement to follow through

During the moments of disengagement, each of which may only last a few seconds in real time, you observe what is transpiring from different perspectives, thereby gaining a more complete understanding of it. It relies upon your PPS—your ability to assess what you are facing and what you are feeling, consider your options, and determine the best course of action.

This is where your role well-being (as described in chapter 6) is a primary source of inner strength. It provides the mental framework to guide you while you reflect on the best way to respond. A simple but effective way to activate this reflective mode is to remember Albert Einstein's quote, "In the middle of difficulty lies opportunity." When you *actively search* for the opportunity that the troubling situation provides you change your mind-set from a reactive mode to a proactive one. Then your capacity to generate a productive response increases.

Practice for Pressure

A more robust method for managing yourself in the face of intense pressure is to develop a set of specific guidelines, rules of engagement, which you practice to the point that they become automatic. The military uses this strategy to make sure that a soldier confronted with a dangerous situation—one that would ordinarily evoke a maladaptive reaction—is able to automatically respond in the best way.

The method is surprisingly simple and effective. It relies on a learned sequence of actions (thoughts and behaviors) combined with *deliberate practice*. It is secured in the subconscious by role playing and visualizing (self-hypnosis) the desired response when confronted with the provocative situation.

Rules of engagement should include the following components:

- get composed
- size up the situation
- determine what needs to be done
- generate a best response
- execute the response

The behavioral and mental steps activate your optimal performance state: the underlying physiological, mental, and emotional mechanisms whereby you feel composed, focused, energized, and able to do whatever is required to meet the challenge. With practice, the rules of engagement become a ritual that, once begun, shifts you from a reactive to a proactive state.

Develop Guidelines for Maintaining Cool under Pressure

The following template can be used for any situation where you want to be sure to able to stay cool. Consider these questions and the example provided as you develop your own rules of engagement.

➢ *When and Where Does the Troublesome Reaction Happen?* Suppose you have a recurrent situation with a customer whom you find immensely frustrating. Each time the customer meets to discuss a purchase, he or she tries to engage you in a repetitive, detailed, and time-consuming review of concerns.

➢ *Identify Your Predictable Automatic Reaction.* Perhaps you feel tension in your chest, get irritable, lose focus, and feel consumed by the feeling that you want to tell this person to cram it and to do business elsewhere.

➤ *What Is the Desired Outcome of Your Response? What Makes This so Important?* The key outcomes you would like to achieve are the customer will feel sufficiently satisfied with your attitude and responses that he will make the purchase and want to remain a regular customer; the customer will respect your time limits and the extent to which you can do justice to his or her concerns.

You need this business and goodwill in the community. You also need to reduce the strain of dealing with this customer so you can return to other matters once the interaction is completed.

➤ *Determine The Ideal Response.* How do you want to respond? What are the specific essential elements your response must contain?

"I will remain composed and in command. My primary focus will be on seeing the situation from his point of view so I can relate to him in a respectful manner. I will be able to clarify, first in my own mind via reflective engagement and then verbally what I can realistically do to satisfy the customer's concerns as CEO and within the time constraints of the meeting."

What key words best capture the qualities you need to have while interacting? Use your list of key words to create a brief narrative that you will use to orient yourself internally. The more specific you are, the more positive impact you gain.

"I will remain calm, composed, and focused on what is most important. I will address concerns in a sincere and respectful way. I will take a slow, deep breath whenever I start to feel tension in my chest. My facial expression will remain pleasant and congenial."

Notice that the focus is on the positive outcomes that you *do* want to happen. This is important. When your self-statements focus on what you will not do, your unconscious hears it as a reminder; you inadvertently remain focused on the negative. Instead, focus on what you *will* do. Then the negative recedes in your mind.

➢ *What specific steps will you take to be certain of responding effectively?*

(1) You must clarify in advance and take full ownership for your responsibility as CEO and the purpose of your interactions with the person.

"I will be prepared to refer him to someone else if he needs more than I can offer, whether it is time or information."

(2) *Formulate the rules of engagement you will follow.*

I.   Before I start approaching the person, I will remember the outcomes that I have identified and the essential components of my desired response. I will say the key guidewords to myself. (Think of the way coaches talk with the team before going on the playing field.)

II. When I first see him, I will remind myself that he is trying to get what is best for his company and that my role is to make the experience go well for him.

III. I will greet him with a cordial smile.

IV. At the onset, I will explain how I can help him, the time we have, and who he can contact if he needs further assistance.

V.   I will remember to use reflective engagement to monitor the process and reformulate responses as needed.

VI. Any time I feel any signs of tension I will pause, take a slow, deep breath, and refocus my goals.

VII. I will reflect back to him each of his concerns to make sure I grasp them correctly and to foster rapport.

(3) *Use deliberate practice to rehearse, clarify, and refine components.*

(4) *Review your performance after the event.*

Reflect on How You Did

Research has shown that *deliberate practice* "when we both do things and then think systematically about what we did, what happened, why those things took place, and how future actions could be different based on those experiences"[95] consolidates learning. Of course for that to happen you must have a growth mind-set: a willingness to admit there is always more to learn coupled with an eagerness to do so.

To improve future performances, it is important that you get at the most crucial components or dimensions of the event. Research[96] demonstrates that the objectives of reflecting are quite similar to those for creating rules of engagement:

- identify the problem,
- analyze the challenge it poses,
- develop a working theory of the problem,
- clarify future actions that should be take.

Use the key questions in figure 10.1 to get the best results. They form the core of the reflective process.

---

1. What happened? (What did you see? What were you feeling? What stood out as the most important aspect?)
2. How is this challenge similar to others you have dealt with?
3. How is this challenge different?
4. What makes this significant for you?
5. What made it happen?
6. How can you do it differently next time for different results?
7. How can you apply this information to guide your future approach?

Adapted from Siebert and Daudelin 1999

Figure 10.1

The results can be compelling. You can go from feeling troubled and bewildered to being calm, poised, and enlightened. It forms the core of a cycle of action and review that allows you to make incremental improvements with experience.

As you acquire more of those kinds of experiences, you build confidence in being able to handle similar pressures. Each time you add to your experience base, you foster the internalized guidelines that allow you to be your own *trusted ally*. Then, when you face a new challenging situation, you know that you can remain cool. You trust that your inner mind will access the framework provided by your role clarity and your accumulated skills. The resulting sense of composure allows you to bring your best ability to the situation, further enhancing the focus you required to reflect on the incoming information and generate a constructive strategy.

Appearing Cool

Another critical aspect of being cool is being able to appear to be cool, even when you are not, as one CEO candidly expressed, "People say we are hard-nosed executives. It's like nothing seems to bother you. Well, you know what? A hell of a lot of stuff seems to bother me; you just don't see it."

Frequently you will be in situations where it is your responsibility to maintain a cool public persona in order to instill a sense of security and hope within others. Jon Coile, president and CEO of Champion Realty, Inc., noted, "The biggest thing you've got to do is hide the stress from everybody else. Because if you exhibit it, they are checking to see, 'Is Dad worried?' And if Dad's worried, they're saying, 'Gee, maybe we should get out of here!'" That makes your problems even worse.

So what happens with the inner struggles that are a natural part of the role? Here again, it is your clear understanding of and ownership for your role that must dominate, even in the face of adversity. This is what enables you to rise above the emotional turmoil. Here's how Charles Sawyer Jr., the managing partner at Meridian Financial Resources, described it: "I built up willpower—a lot of it is personal strength—you have to take a deep breath and talk to yourself and get tough."

Talking to oneself was a common theme among the project participants. Tom Darrow, SPHR, founder and principal at Talent Connections, LLC, and Career Spa, LLC, finds it helpful to come back to two adages: "Never let 'em see you sweat," and "Always behave like a duck: remain calm and unruffled on the surface, but paddle like the devil underneath."

It is noteworthy that two of the eight leadership principles of Nelson Mandela[97] relate to managing one's appearance and the importance of displaying courage in the face of adversity.

In 1994, during the presidential-election campaign, Mandela got on a tiny propeller plane to fly down to the killing fields of Natal and give a speech to his Zulu supporters. I agreed to meet him at the airport, where we would continue our work after his speech. When the plane was twenty minutes from landing, one of its engines failed. Some on the plane began to panic. The only thing that calmed them was looking at Mandela, who quietly read his newspaper as if he were a commuter on his morning train to the office. The airport prepared for an emergency landing, and the pilot managed to land the plane safely. When Mandela and I got in the backseat of his bulletproof BMW that would take us to the rally, he turned to me and said, "Man, I was terrified up there!" (Stengel 2008)

Make It Happen

Step One. Identify a recurring situation that has challenged your ability to remain cool. Choose a situation that occurs often enough to get in some good practice over the next few weeks. Be sure to clarify what you hope to gain by improving how you handle it.

Step Two. Develop your rules of engagement for the next occurrence of this situation using the guidelines offered in this chapter. Consider the next occurrence of this situation an opportunity to try out your new approach!

Step Three. Use the reflection questions to assess your performance after the next occurrence of this situation. Then revise your goals as needed each time you deal with this challenging situation over the next two weeks. As you see growth in your competence at remaining cool, you can apply this method to other situations.

Chapter 11

RECOVERING YOUR COOL

A great diver learns to stand down his emotions.
At the moment he becomes lost or blinded or tangled or trapped ...
he dials down his fear and contracts into the moment until his breathing slows ...
and his reason returns.

—Robert Kurson, *Shadow Divers*

No matter how good you are at staying cool, there will be times when the right combination of stressors converges and you *will* lose your composure. You will experience *distress* and find yourself in a reactive mode. At such times, you need the equivalent of a skydiver's safety chute: backup, surefire methods to recover quickly and to minimize the potential damages.

As CEO, your capacity to reliably recover from loss of cool prevents bottom-line company losses that are tied to

Morale—Negativity adds to staff tension, undermines company spirit, and diminishes the overall enthusiasm that otherwise leads employees to put forth their best efforts.
Company Culture—Your behavior is the model for how to handle difficult situations within your company, and you will see it reflected throughout the work environment.
Health—Chronic distress from working in an environment where stress regularly boils over adds to the risk of medical problems among the staff as their bodies are continually bathed in stress hormones.

Test pilot Chuck Yeager[98] was the epitome of someone who possessed the skills to recover quickly from an acutely distressing situation. Consider the day that he climbed into an experimental aircraft for a supersonic test flight. All was fine until the plane suddenly began to spin out of control and plummet through the sky. Imagine what he went through as he realized his position and the likelihood of a fatal crash. Yet he regained control of the aircraft and landed safely. What went on in his mind and body that enabled him to harness his ability to focus his efforts on just what was needed? Most of us untrained mortals would have remained panic stricken. That's why we love our real-life and movie heroes. They epitomize *cool!*

In the business world, we regularly face less dramatic, yet intensely gripping, circumstances that push us past our limits. The resulting feelings of alarm, urgency, and overwhelm can easily override our good judgment. This, of course, is what we refer to as being "stressed out." We lose our cool.

Distress can wreak havoc with the basic operations of a business. This happened at a well-established, upscale restaurant during the depths of the 2009 recession. Marla, the general manager of the restaurant, consulted with me when the owner, Art, went from understandably troubled to short-tempered and difficult to deal with. His worry was getting the upper hand, and he lost his usual poised manner. His distress oozed into his interactions with Marla. He questioned and challenged the way she managed the operation, first in private and then in front of other staff. Art's behavior deteriorated to the point that he picked on the kitchen and wait staff about tiny details. Glaring at one of the servers who made a minor mistake, he yelled, "Why did you do that? You are so stupid!" A few times his insults were made in front of other servers, once even within earshot of customers.

Soon the grumbling among the servers changed to talk of quitting. They became irritable and complained to each other and to Marla about the stressful work environment. Several of the servers left precipitously. Art rebuffed Marla's multiple efforts to collaborate on a strategy for making things better. She eventually realized staying in this toxic environment was futile. She left her position for one in a restaurant where the owner had a track record of treating staff with consideration and respect, even during that challenging economic time.

Desperate to change the situation for the better, Art paradoxically destroyed the morale and culture of the restaurant. He crossed over the line from being appropriately *fierce*—strong and quick to take decisive action under duress—to being *aggressive.*[99] Understandable? Sure. Acceptable? No!

What are the implications for you? Your determination to take full ownership for being a CEO requires that you align yourself with the take-charge Hardiness for Hard Times approach. You must develop strategies and skills, like the ones below, that equip you to effectively manage those inevitable times when you lose your composure.

Events That Trigger Loss of Cool

Sometimes loss of cool happens all at once due to a single, drastic event. More often, though, loss of cool happens as various pressures build and available resources become depleted—the proverbial "straw that broke the camel's back." One CEO described the experience of emotional and mental overwhelm as a time "when all four corners of life are demanding something big from me—when family, work, and other obligations all combine."

Even though loss of cool is a function of mental and emotional factors, usually one or the other is more prominent. Let's briefly consider each one.

Emotional Overload

Just as a gymnast is more likely to be upset by a broken ankle than a software programmer would be, we can predict certain key triggers of emotional upheaval for a CEO. Of course it is also true that the emotional impact of an event can have unique meaning due to your life experiences and personal realities. We focus here on a few of the most common types of events that can trigger an emotional meltdown.

- **You made a bad administrative decision.** You realize your decision, action, or inaction was faulty, cannot be undone, and may hurt the company or a key business alliance. The consequences for the company are potentially large. Your competence will be questioned.
- **Someone you depended upon was neglectful or inept.** This is the most frequently cited source of frustration for executives that I hear. In order for you to do your job, you must rely on individuals and departments to do their part. Discovering a staff member or a department did an inadequate job can be absolutely infuriating.

- **Convergence of multiple interpersonal demands.** Direct pressures from important people add an emotional dimension to any matter. You may receive urgent requests from several staff members in close succession, or you may experience work demands and personal pressures that conflict. Your eagerness to please, or fear of disappointing or offending the other person, can intensify the pressure.

Mental Overload

Just as your computer is likely to freeze up when you try to run too many programs at once, sometimes concurrent demands can overload your information processing capacity. At these times, you may experience a sort of mental tangle that shows itself as an inability to think through all the components of the situation and to generate a viable strategy. You may find yourself having difficulty grasping the complexity of the event or with developing a strategy that can lead to a comprehensive solution. After all, sometimes you are called upon to resolve a problem that is unfamiliar, bigger, or more complex than you have previously encountered, or to generate a strategy under excessive time and resource pressures.

Following are common triggers of mental overload for CEOs.

- **Schedule Changes.** You can easily slip into feeling overloaded when an unexpected and important event disrupts the plan you have so diligently set up. For example, you've done a thorough job planning your week to assure you will meet several important project goals. An abrupt schedule change imposed by the representative of a major business ally throws the plan into disarray. You have to reconfigure your plan.
- **Loss of Essential Resources.** A crisis may be precipitated by the loss of a major revenue source, breakdown in technology, or the loss of a key player. Such breakdowns in a vital component of the operating system can have far-reaching disruptive consequences. The interruption to business as usual can create a crisis situation that ripples through the organization, requiring quick and creative solutions that are congruent with the integrity of the business.

For example, in the midst of setting up a major project one of your key staff members is unexpectedly not able to continue in her pivotal role. There is no backup person who can seamlessly step in, so this loss creates an enormous disruption to the project. It is essential that you revise the strategy in short order, including finding and integrating a new person into the team.

Disruptive Reactions to Events

When our emotions or our internal information processors are overwhelmed, there are predictable experiences and effects. Understanding these can help as you consider strategies for recovering from a loss of cool.

Emotional Turmoil

You likely know raw emotion can disrupt your ability to respond constructively in a crisis. However, the intensity and speed with which this can come on can be a surprise.

This was deeply impressed upon me many years ago during my first kayak outing. On the drive there, my friend Doug gave instructions on how to handle the challenges I might encounter. We arrived at the designated spot, and Doug helped me squirm the lower half of my body into the classic kayak's small opening.

I successfully paddled through the initial rapids, and then I pulled into a small cove to rest. I was sitting perfectly still in the kayak when all of a sudden it flipped over. Stunned, I twisted my body and could see the surface of the water and the sky above, but my body was "stuck" in the kayak. I panicked and thrashed about. Realizing I could not free myself, Doug righted the boat. Then he revealed that he had snuck up behind me and deliberately flipped it in order to give me the "opportunity" to learn how to get myself out of a kayak if it overturned.

Once out of the immediate crisis, I soon recovered my rational thinking. Then the way to manage a flipped kayak was obvious to me. If I had been able to get my wits about me at the time, I could have immediately focused on calming myself for a few seconds. That would have allowed me to remember how I had gotten into the kayak (relax your body and slither in). Thus, seeing how to liberate myself from the "entrapment" would have been easy (relax your body and slither out!).

Afterward, the realization of how easily I could lose presence of mind and become stuck in a totally *reactive mode* scared me. I had been unable to think constructively. I was blinded by feelings of overwhelm (fears of catastrophe). I had no access to my ability to think practically about the demands of the situation because the desperate effort to seek immediate escape consumed me.

I learned important lessons from my kayak outing, and I am grateful for them now. However, I was not pleased at the time. I was embarrassed and angry with my friend for deliberately putting me in that situation. We all need to watch out for the emotions that can come after a loss of cool, even when in less dramatic situations. Some people launch into a self-blaming character assassination that leaves them consumed with self-doubt, self-contempt, guilt, anxiety, or even panic. Others may move into a blaming mode and feel determined to exact revenge.

What I finally took away from the experience was this: the narrowed thinking that occurred when raw emotion took over in that kayak was counterproductive. I vowed to learn failsafe methods for modulating my emotions and disrupting the knee-jerk reactions that can ambush constructive thinking.

Likewise, getting trapped by your reactive mode is distinctly counter to the objectives you as a CEO must have. Successful CEOs master the art of quickly recovering their cool so they can operate in *responsive mode,* allowing for active constructive thinking.

Surely that's how Chuck Yeager operated in the cockpit of his test planes. You can too.

Mental Chaos

Like an overloaded computer, sometimes demands overwhelm the resources of your brain, and your mental processing becomes inefficient and erratic. You may find your mind jumps from one aspect of the problem to another and that you cycle repeatedly through the same jumbled and tangled web of ideas. You may sense or suspect that there are crucial factors that you cannot grasp, and that it is difficult to organize the components to be solved into a cohesive and manageable framework. You may get stuck in feeling the enormity of the problem and thinking about implications that are so big and complex that you cannot trust yourself to generate a satisfactory strategy.

Consider Janet's situation. Her deadline for completing the company's five-year plan for the board of directors was fast approaching. She carefully planned her schedule for the next couple of days and was confident that she could pull it off if she diligently stuck to her schedule. Then one of her department heads called to say there was a critical breakdown in one of the production plants. The delayed production schedule would hold up delivery of an order for a major account that was already threatening to move its business elsewhere. Already concerned about how her board of directors viewed her performance for the last year, the implications of the potential loss of another major account were a grave concern.

Janet's mind frantically raced from one concern to another, as her chest tensed and her breathing became labored. She felt trapped—gripped by the stress reaction. How nice it would have been if she was skilled in some of the following methods!

Rules of Engagement for Managing Loss of Cool

In chapter 10, you learned that rules of engagement specify the circumstances under which you will engage specific resources. Let's briefly define the rules of engagement related to regaining your cool, and then we will turn to building a repertoire of practiced and trusted skills that you can call upon when it is time to engage.

General Principles

The purpose of your rules of engagement is to assure the following outcomes:

> ➤ rapid recovery of access to internal resources,
> ➤ maintenance of positive relationships,
> ➤ quick resumption of normal work mode.

Remember, the distress alarm is automatic. It resides in the lower brain stem, which is not normally under the control of the upper brain's capacity for self-regulating. So how can you bring more conscious control to this process? Throughout the book you have read about the importance of self-monitoring and have learned ways to do so. That perspective and skill set will serve you well.

Self-Monitoring. You need to observe the signs in your body, mind, emotions, and behavior that signal that you are losing your cool in order to know when to engage your skills for self-management. It is the physiological cues that result from the distress alarm that may be the first sign you have lost your cool. You may notice your heart is pounding, your breathing is rapid, your hands are perspiring, and your whole body tense. For one professional, it was when her forehead felt furrowed and tight and her voice came through clenched teeth that she knew she was in distress mode.

Or you might notice you are talking faster and louder or having trouble getting words out at all. Perhaps you are snapping at your staff or grumbling to yourself. Cognitively, you may notice you are distracted and having trouble sticking with the work that needs to be done.

Your response to the distress alarm, if unchecked, can lead to a cascade of events:

➢ You fail to recognize that you are losing your cool or you misread the extent of your distress.
➢ You become gripped by whatever is upsetting you.
➢ You are distracted from the work that needs to be done.
➢ You spread turmoil to others by operating in reactive mode in your work and personal relationships.

Offsetting this automatic progression of reactions, good self-monitoring provides you with the information you need in order to recognize that it is time to engage methods to regain your cool. These will guide you back to your normal capacity to work effectively.

General Components of Effective Recovery Methods

The cornerstone of your recovery strategy must include a repertoire of methods to:

• Reduce escalation: you must be able to *create a buffer* between yourself and the source of distress.

- Regain control: it is imperative that you move quickly to *take charge.*

CFO Ed Kelley, who takes pride in not being "a person who explodes and falls over," summarized the process of regaining his cool: "There are times I must take some moments to press the relief valve, physically and emotionally, so I can address the crisis that is building. I have to not react with an in-kind reaction. I have to get calmer within and take the steps so I can really bring a solution to whatever it is that is causing the distress."

In the remainder of this chapter, you will find a variety of methods that can help you as you learn to recover from situations when you have lost your cool.

As with any effort to change your own behavior, your attitude sets the stage for how you approach the learning, and it is a key to good outcomes. *Losing your cool is not about you as a person.* It is not evidence of a character defect. Rather, it is the human version of an electrical system blowing a fuse or a computer locking up—the outcome of your mental and/or emotional systems being overloaded. So, you need a software upgrade that will provide you with the skills required to handle the load. This nonjudgmental perspective makes it easier for you to eliminate the common pitfalls of self-recrimination, tirades against others, and needing to "appear" to be cool when you really are not. Then you can be free to learn, and you will obtain the best and most expedient results for you and the organization.

Strategies

There is no single "best" strategy or sequence of strategies to regain control when you have lost your cool. You will need to become familiar with a variety of strategies that work for you so you can select the best one depending on the specific circumstances.

I have organized the information by category, including emotional and mental strategies, and from the simplest to the most complex. The emotional strategies aim to disrupt and calm the flooding of emotional and bodily energy. The mental tactics focus on disrupting and regaining control of narrowed thinking and distorted cognition. In the real world, you will find that these strategies overlap and work together to guide you back to your usual cool manner of operating.

Emotional Strategies

Do a Soft Reboot

Like a soft reboot when your computer is jammed, a well-practiced, quick release ritual interrupts the reactive response in your mind and body. This enables you to regain sufficient control to refocus on a constructive response to the problem. The key component is a behavioral action that calms the body. It is in situations like this where a simple relaxation method, such as the 4-8-8 breathing method described in chapter 5, is ideal. Another technique is to simply take a slow deep breath, let it out slowly and then repeat to yourself a meaningful phrase, such as, "Be cool, man."

Top Gun jet pilot Captain Jeffrey Winter was taught that when an emergency happens in the cockpit, "The first thing you should do is wind your clock." He acknowledged that it "seems really silly, but the idea is, don't freak out." The intent is to make certain you "don't shoot before you aim."

Scream. That's Right, Scream! (Vent!)

Sometimes, you just need to release the pressure valve and let off some steam. Matthew described an especially upsetting situation when his administrative assistant told him she had just received a message that the new hire for a key position was not going to work out. "The only thing I could do was walk away, shut the door, and scream. I screamed. I slammed my fists on my desk. Then I took a couple of deep breaths, got control of myself, went back, and I was fine. The stress relief was just the primal scream to get it out."

Roger, a COO, had a boss he described as "frustration personified." He developed a strategy for times when the frustration threatened to overwhelm him. Roger explained that he walked into an inactive storeroom next to his office and "screamed at the top of my lungs and no one would hear me. I would do that some days once or twice, other days not at all."

It should go without stating that you must use the utmost of discretion when screaming. Automobiles offer one of the very best places.

Have a Good Cry

While some feel the need to scream, others find that a good cry offers the release that they need. Alice either closes her office door or goes into the ladies room so she can cry. "I let myself cry, until I don't feel like it anymore. I wash my face and then do a breathing exercise to regain my composure."

Similarly, another executive noted how she sometimes needs to allow herself the opportunity to feel her feelings with full-on intensity: "Instead of trying to deny it, for a brief period of time, I immerse myself in it, let myself feel it, and contemplate on it. And then when I come back, I feel strong. I'm ready to go."

In Case of Fire, Take the Nearest Exit

Remember the "Get out of jail free" card in the Monopoly game? Escaping or eluding a difficulty is your "Get out of jail free" card. Keep one tucked away for when you need it the most. Getting out of your office may be just what you need to distract your attention from the turmoil in order to break its grip.

One CEO escapes by taking the elevator to the top floor of his office building, and then he walks down the stairs. I also know a CEO who walks around the inside of the building so he can engage staff in light social interchanges. Emory Mulling, founder and chairman of the Mulling Corporation, takes a diversion by stepping out of the office.

> I'll go to the cafeteria and get a V8 or something, just to get away from it. Then I'll think about good stuff, like my plans for enjoying the evening, or what kind of exercising I'm going to do. The main thing is you've got to release the hold it has on you. Then you can go back, and it is not as bad as you thought it was.

One executive walks to a nearby store to get a soda; another sits in the corner booth of a nearby restaurant "to help me chill." Then he quietly reflects on the distressing matters to figure things out and to set a course for the next day and the coming week.

Seek Refuge in Your "Cave"

Closing the office door for privacy is the preferred strategy for some when strong emotions kick in. Make it a place of solitude by shutting down all outside connections. Turn off all electronic devices. Put down your papers.

In addition to regaining your composure, this onsite retreat helps with damage control, decreasing the chances that you will do or say something you might regret. Here is how Bill Hickman, a leadership trainer and coach, does it.

> I shut down temporarily. I physically remove myself from the situation, shut the door, and breathe as deeply and as slowly as I can to try and get some equilibrium.

Similarly, Janet doesn't like to "knee-jerk react to anything because then you're never going to see clearly. Your perception is going to be skewed." To preserve her image as an effective leader, she has learned the importance of finding a way to get out of view when upset so she can "just go and get it out of my system. When I can let myself feel it under my terms, then I can put it behind me."

Put on the Salve

Sometimes you need a calming activity that is absorbing enough to pull you away from the matters at hand. More time-intensive than the soft reboot releases described earlier in this chapter, relaxation techniques such as meditation and yoga (see chapter 4) are especially efficient and powerful methods that pull your attention into your body in a way that is similar to getting into a hot tub, triggering the body's physiological relaxation response.

Some professionals find that using a visualization strategy does the trick. "I lean back in the chair, close my eyes, and take maybe ten minutes to do nothing but reflect about the beach, the mountains, the movie I saw last night, or something that would take my mind totally away from where I was."

You can also engage in nonwork activities such as reading a novel, listening to music, or playing an electronic game. Nature walks are especially effective for self-calming. Here is how Linda Schuett, managing lawyer of Anne Arundel County Government, expressed it.

> There's something about looking at the sky and the clouds and the trees that makes me feel very connected to the universe. And when I'm in that place, all of the things that get on my nerves are diminished as I determine whether my level of distress is really warranted given the nature of the issue, in comparison to life as a whole.

Call a Time Out

Sports teams know the value of a strategic time out. Similarly, Donald Treinen, copresident of Alliance Plus, Inc., noted:

> You must master the ability to take a time out: to slow down, to relax, to take a deep breath, just to give yourself a time buffer. A person needs to have some disengagement from the thing that is causing the stress, even if it's only for five minutes.

Time outs allow you to recover physical and emotional energy, get perspective on the situation, and formulate a strategy for the return to action.

Lean on Someone

There are times when what is needed is not advice but an empathic listener to lighten the emotional load. "When I go home, it's talking to my wife, a couple of good friends, or occasionally my daughter. It's the equilibrium that comes from checking in with them."

Turn to a Higher Power

Turning to prayer, in addition to the support they get from others, is helpful for some executives, such as CEO and president of the Keyes Company, Mike Pappas.

Sometimes, I'll say, "Hey, there's got to be a bigger picture. I need help." And I'll ask for help ... I ask for wisdom. I ask for comfort. I ask for strength. I get in the car or a private place and I'll actually hold my hand up and say, "Hold my hand."

Take an off-Site Retreat

There are times when you are so gripped by the upset that you need to get even further away. In order to recover, you may need further separation from the heat of battle, a break in the physical connection to the workplace, and an opportunity to release the physical and emotional tension.

When "all the king's horses and all the king's men cannot put humpty dumpty back together," it may be best to leave work for the day. Some just go home, and some go shopping. Some go for a long walk on the beach, a stroll around a park, or go swimming, jogging, or biking.

When I get that stressed out, I do get to a point where I just stop what I'm doing, walk away, and go home. I've found that to be much more productive than trying to sit here and figure it out. I may sit in the hot tub. I may go for a walk. I might go see the children.

Danger Ahead: Proceed with Caution

When there is insufficient time to regain your cool before the next scheduled meeting, you must proceed cautiously. One executive described her decision tree for handling meetings at these times. If the meeting is unrelated to the troublesome topic, she is more confident that she can remain levelheaded.

What helps is that we're talking about something that has nothing to do with the subject that makes me upset. If it is related to what has made me upset, I will probably cancel out of the meeting, because I wouldn't be able to discuss it.

In those situations, she has her administrative assistant get her out of the meeting before it happens.

145

And if she is in the meeting or with the person and the troublesome issue comes up? She has a rehearsed phrase. "I'm not able to meet with you right now about this, because there's something else going on for me and I need to be by myself."

Mental Strategies

The strategies we have discussed so far focus on ways to disrupt the flood of emotions and calm the body. Now we turn to methods that help you regain your cool by working with your thinking process. These are designed to bring you back to a clearer head and better access to your best abilities.

Get a Grip on Yourself

Talking to yourself is often jokingly described as a sure sign that you are losing your grip. From a self-regulation perspective, though, it may be just what you need to *get* a grip! After slowing and stabilizing your mind and emotions, you can take charge by having a talk with yourself. Let's listen in on some of the conversations that executives described having in the privacy of their own heads.

Don Treinen tells himself:

This is okay. It is not what I planned. If I'd have planned this it wouldn't have happened this way or at this time. But my involvement is essential, so I've got to adjust my thinking to embrace this new situation.

The first thing you need to do is just recognize you've messed up and accept the fact that, "Okay, I made a bad decision, wrong decision, let me see what I can go do to fix it." Don't be thickheaded and stubborn about it because it only gets worse. Move quickly, admit you've made a decision and move forward.

A typically unflappable CEO described how she uses a pet phrase to focus her mind combined with a behavioral action to calm down: "When there is something that really kind of feels like it's knocking your socks off, or you know that you're just getting more excited than you need to be and you know it's ridiculous, I just say, 'Hang on here one second!' and stop to take in a deep breath. It reminds me, 'Okay, this is really nuts here, just hang on!'"

Stop Wallowing and Rise to the Occasion

When the pep talk is not sufficient, there comes a point where you've got to get fed up with feeling sorry for yourself or blaming others. You can help yourself to regain presence of mind, "bite the bullet," and take responsibility for doing whatever it takes to move on and deal with the situation.

Here's how Charles Sawyer Jr. helps himself get past blaming others and takes back ownership for his responsibility. "I talk to myself in my mind. I believe in a very simple philosophy that there are three kinds of people. I tell myself that there are people who make things happen, people that let things happen to them, people that are not sure what the hell happened. So I always go back to that. This happened in the past; I have to fix it; I have to solve the problem."

Call in Your "Defense Attorney"

Do you have an inner "prosecuting attorney" that floods you with accusations and indictments over your missteps? Such prosecuting attorneys can be ruthless in their assaults on your character or competency. Force yourself to take the stance of your "defense attorney." Mount a defense on your own behalf by making yourself look at what went wrong from alternate perspectives to dispute the "facts" of what happened and any distortions in the evaluation of your competency.

For example, your "prosecuting attorney/inner critic" may be attesting that you had more than ample time to complete a proposal, and that the consequence of not submitting one on time is that your company's revenues will fall far short of the Board of Directors' expectations. Furthermore, your failure is evidence that you lack leadership skills the company needs. When you switch to the defense attorney's perspective, you point out that, in fact, you made a choice to put your time into a far more important project, and that the benefits of that initiative have greater long-term benefits to the company than the one you did not complete.

Pull out Your Secret Copy of *The Idiot's Guide to Dealing with Mental Overload*

A structured routine can be handy to steer your efforts toward a constructive strategy. Having a template for dealing with the situation can sidestep the muddled thinking of the moment. In Chapter 10, you learned about strategies for building behavioral routines that can help prevent loss of cool. Here, we look at ways you can also use behavioral routines to build better habits for situations when you have already lost your cool. Below are some examples of templates that executives have used. Feel free to borrow from them or create your own.

Template for Loss of Cool. The following six-step ritual helps CEO Clinton Wingrove when he's feeling completely thrown off-center.

(1) Take a deep breath to initiate calmness and help yourself step back.
(2) Acknowledge what happened.
(3) Write down the thoughts that are streaming through your mind about what happened. Repeat as needed over a day or so.
(4) Put the whole matter completely aside for at least twenty-four hours. Do not focus on it directly, unless there are external demands that must be dealt with.
(5) Return to the notes for reflection. Does what you thought about and wrote down and reflected on still make sense?
(6) Formulate a final response and move into action.

System to Eliminate Churning. CIO Pete Stark developed the following template to guide himself out of his tendency to get stuck in churning. His objective here is to shift to a reflective mode, regain perspective, take control, and foster closure.

(1) Get the issue onto a post-it note.
(2) Determine the amount of time it will take to address the issue. Immediately schedule the time to deal with it by putting it into your calendar just as you would any meeting.
(3) Schedule double the amount of time than what you think you will need.

(4) Determine the appropriate person(s) required to act on the issue. Put only the one item on the table. Decide in advance what is it you want yourself or others to take away from the meeting.

(5) Concentrate on the staff person's accountability and what it takes for that person to be successful, as appropriate.

(6) Keep the discussion focused on the outcome and the tasks needed to get there.

(7) If there is a problem with the outcome, address it right away. Make the time. Do not set it aside.

Use Brainstorming

Once you have made it through the onslaught of the storm, it's time to shift your focus to a different and much more positive metaphorical storm—a brainstorm. Once you have your wits about you, shift into a problem-solving mode. Generate as many possible solutions as you can to whatever knocked you off center.

Here is how Donald Treinen captured the essence of what you are trying to accomplish.

> When you're faced with an urgent situation, you don't go from pausing to action. The first thing to do is to focus on, "What is the problem?" You take time to reflect on the situation—to think about it, to kind of walk around it and look at it from different angles, to get other kinds of perspectives about what's involved.
>
> Then quickly move to, "What are your possible solutions?" This is in contrast to just dwelling on the problem itself. It's not just, "I've got a problem." But, "Okay, I've got a problem. Here's what the problem is. What are my possible solutions?"

Don described the process of moving into brainstorming mode in this way. "Okay, what do I know about this situation? What do I need to learn? What unique capabilities do I have that enable me to be involved in it? What is my responsibility here? Who else is involved and how can we work together to most effectively and efficiently get whatever it is that needs to be done completed?"

Be Mentally Flexible

A natural part of feeling overwhelmed is a sense of urgency—it feels as if the sky will fall unless you quickly resolve the matter. The result, like with my kayaking experience, is that your focus narrows and this can lead you to become mentally rigid. You may need a strategy to interrupt these tendencies.

Here is a three-step strategy to regain mental flexibility.

1. Remind yourself there *are* ways to deal with almost all situations.
2. Ask yourself a powerful focusing question, such as, "How can I look at this situation so I can see a way to start managing it?"
3. Shift to the new constructive vantage point.

Ed Kelley reported that he found it helpful to start by asking himself, "How critical is this incident that is causing this stress?" He went on to describe the conversation he has with himself to shift his way of looking at the situation.

It must be put into the perspective that, yes, it is troublesome. It's a grain of sand in the oyster, and we are going to overcome it because we can overcome it. We have the techniques within ourselves and we have resources around us to use to overcome this stress. We could put that in place immediately, so the stress does not build to the disabling point.

Finding a new vantage point may require some advance mapping. Here are some "landmarks" that you can feed into your PPS when you need to access a location that will give you a different perspective on the distressing event.

Accept That Stuff Happens

One executive explained that over time, experience has brought him greater ability to anchor himself. "As you get older, you know this too shall pass. So you just say to yourself, 'There's nothing I can do. This particular area is out of my control, and I'm just going to let it go.' That can be easier said than done, but it helps to at least take myself through that exercise and get my mind to acknowledge that I do have to let it go."

Wadi Rahim, president at AmDyne Corporation, who had successfully guided his company through a major legal and financial crisis, described it this way. "When I have two or three critical problems with no solutions, I will stop and do a 'control-alt-delete' and reset. Then I'm able to recognize this is only a company. Once I return to that perspective, I realize that I'm not going to die and my family is not. Then I readdress the problem as a problem—not a life or death challenge to me personally."

Face and Fight Your Worst Fears

Some people find that they can reduce the gravity of a situation by looking at it from the perspective of their worst-case scenario. They identify different options for the scenario to get to a more comfortable point.

Chris Coile, founder and chairman of the board at Champion Realty, Inc., who had been through two major upheavals with his real estate business, shared this perspective.

> You ask, "What if the worst happened?" Let's say you can lose your job, $300,000, and you close the company down. Or the guy that you're worried about leaves you and takes some other people.

> I ask myself, "What would I do?" And then I'd figure it out. I don't mind starting something fresh, doing something new. Once I realize that the worst that can happen to me isn't all that bad, I can deal with it.

Been There, Done That

A helpful way to mobilize your self-confidence is to review prior experiences when you faced similar challenges as the current one and handled them well.

Here is how early trial by fire became a source of self-confidence for Carolyn B. Elman, CEO of American Business Women's Association.

I was just in my third year as head of the organization and in charge of the national meeting. I was working with a consultant, who was a liar. She just lied! She said she did research that she didn't do and pitted managers against each other. It was amazing.

Before I recognized it, I took her advice as opposed to the advice of the convention manager. Along with that, the five thousand members came to Kansas City upset about the recent dues increase and changes in materials. And nobody likes change. And who was this woman anyway—meaning me!

Then the meeting happened. We had a disaster of a banquet. Some of it was uncontrollable. It rained the entire time, so people were getting on and off buses in the rain. Well, I mean, the stars were not aligned. So I had five thousand people very angry with me.

Once I figured out how to get through that, I realized there wasn't really any disaster I didn't feel like I could manage. Two years away from that it was like, "Okay, bring it on!" This is nothing worse than what I've already been through.

Reframe as an Opportunity

Once you engage your mind in searching for what good can come from a crisis, you can find the opportunity that leads to positive change and to renewed energy. You shift from feeling out of control to feeling in charge. For example, the loss of a key contract due to poor quality control could point to the value of tightening up on a monitoring procedure, leading to a better performance for future contracts, as Phil Soucy, founder, copresident and CEO at Modern Technology Solutions, Inc., pointed out.

Sometimes at the moment things can feel like, "Oh my god! This person is a key person. She is telling me that she is planning on leaving ..." Then I remind myself that the last time that happened, it turned out to work out for the better. Because we hired two people, and they came in and took us to the next level.

Reframe in Context of Priorities

Find a higher mountain and look at the situation with a longer view. When you step back from the immediacy of a distressing problem and see it in the larger framework of your goals, the picture changes.

For example, Bill Hickman noted that sometimes he realizes that he's gotten mired in the details, is going from crisis to crisis, and has lost the big picture. To get back to his ability to plan for the longer-term, he finds it helps to say to himself, "Stop. Keep in mind what you are trying to accomplish. Don't go down the rabbit holes!" Then he asks, "What is the most important thing? What am I trying to accomplish? Why am I doing what I'm doing?" From his new viewpoint, he can return to the situation with more flexibility.

Consulting Strategies

The story is told that the real reason that the Jews wandered the desert for forty days and nights is because none of the men would ask for directions. Not the most flattering view of men, I know, but it is a reminder that it takes a real "man" to know his or her limits and to know when and whom to ask for help. Because of the high risk of disruption from losing your cool, it is essential that you have excellent options for enlisting support from others.

Have a Virtual Consult with a Revered Leader. Free up your mind and seek inspiration and insight by wondering how your favorite leaders would handle the situation. How would Jack Welch, Andrew Carnegie, or Peter Drucker manage the situation? In this way, you can enlist Napoleon Hill's[100] method of consulting an imaginary board of directors comprised of the business experts you most admire.

Use the Buddy System. A buddy[101] can be a particularly important safety mechanism when you are trying to recover from a loss of cool. A trusted colleague that you can turn to when you are floundering can help you regain a better perspective. Carl, a company president, described how he seeks his trusted buddy within the company in this way. "I can be pretty dark, and can head down a road where one negative builds on the other. And that's when I need somebody else to say, 'How many of those dominos are going to fall the way you're saying they're going to fall?'"

He went on to explain that his COO is another person he can turn to when he needs to bring out the whole scenario. Knowing he tends to fall prey to his own temper, he has learned to seek a reality check. "Am I overreacting here? How big is this issue? What do you think I need to do?"

Seek Consultation. Some people find that it is helpful to formalize a relationship with a mentor, coach, or advisory group. The consultant becomes a vital team member who can empathize with the feelings of overwhelm, give advice, and facilitate a problem-solving approach.

Likewise, when a crisis disrupts an essential business plan, it is often prudent to seek advice from your operational team. Paul Silber, PhD, president, CEO, and founder at In Vitro Technologies, Inc., likened the challenge to a sports team.

> You know if you fumble the ball, you say, "Okay, let's put the best team on the field that we can." Whether it is a personnel issue and someone's got to leave the company, or someone has resigned unexpectedly who is a key person, or we've just upset an important customer, we will regroup as a team by getting the interested parties into a room together. We say, "Okay, we've got a serious problem ... Now, how do we resolve this issue? Where do we go from here?"

Getting Closure without Closing Yourself Off

The objective of these strategies for recovering from a loss of cool event is, of course, to quickly regain your capacity for normal work performance and to maintain positive relationships. When you get back in the game you want to be fully ready to play ball. However, it is important to be aware of a common pitfall. In your eagerness to move on from whatever triggered your loss of cool, you may minimize the significance of the triggering event. Before you put the situation behind you, be sure that you are not overlooking important lessons. Are there changes that you can make that will make it less likely that you will lose your cool in the future? Are there protocols or operating procedures that need to change? For example, one CEO noted that his loss of cool was triggered by an urgent call from his son in the middle of a workday. So he came up with a plan to deal with similar matters in the future to minimize the disruption.

Remember, too, that every event when you lose your cool is an opportunity to improve your coping skills using the guidelines for self-improvement in chapter 3. Every crisis begets opportunity!

Make It Happen

Step One. Identify your biggest weakness in managing your emotions. When do you tend to lose your cool? What are your triggers? How does this impact your effectiveness and the operation of your business?

Step Two. Select one emotional strategy that best fits with your personal style. When can you practice the strategy? Remember that practice is a part of retraining yourself as you learn to interrupt your characteristic emotional and physiological responses. Set specific and realistic goals.

Step Three. Select one mental strategy described in this chapter that suits your cognitive style and needs. As noted above, you will need practice for new ways of thinking to automatically kick in when you have lost your cool. Focus on specific and realistic goals for incorporating the strategy into your repertoire.

Section IV

MANAGING THE WORK DAY

The interviews for the CEO Stress Project all started with the same question: "On a typical day, do you actively think about how to manage stress?" To my surprise, most said no. I soon realized the participants understood the term "stress" to mean being overwhelmed, and these CEOs do not typically experience a sense of overwhelm. So, I thought, okay, how about feeling "bogged down?" Surely dealing with the people and managing the tasks they face every day must feel like a weight. I began to use the term "bogged down" in my probes of participants' initial responses. What I discovered is that these masters at managing pressures tend to view all their daily tasks and dealings with people as just part of the workday—their daily grind. It is not distressing, nor does it make them feel weighed down; they expect it and it is all part of the job. Over the course of each interview, aspects of their roles that felt challenging did appear—the most salient was people. However, the day-to-day tasks were not on that list.

Most of the participants had perspectives and strategies that buffered a sense of distress. It is notable that the more seasoned the executive the more likely they were to have well-established and effective ways of handling the daily tasks and more wisdom for dealing with matters in general. For several of them I had to ask that they recall earlier phases when they did experience distress! Perhaps their insights can set you on the same course.

Overview of Section

In this section, we focus on how to deal with the daily grind. The following two chapters focus on those aspects of dealing with the daily grind that I believe will give you the greatest return on your efforts. Once again, my focus is on the key contact points that occur between you and what you are doing. The power to improve how you handle the pressures of your day comes from leveraging these points. Use them now to improve your ability to manage your workday, and consider them a resource if you find you need a refresher.

Chapter 12, Managing Relationships, offers guidelines for how to build and maintain the vital relationships within your work world. You will find ways to increase your people skills and reduce your distress while gaining in overall effectiveness.

Chapter 13, Managing Workflow, covers strategies to manage daily tasks and demands. We will consider ways to build filters that allow you to sort and prioritize tasks and your role in dealing with them, allowing you to focus on your critical leadership functions.

Chapter 12

MANAGING RELATIONSHIPS

*The most important area of growth I've seen in my career
is working with and through people
as opposed to simply trying to be a one-armed paper hanger.*

—Frank Slocumb

The most frequently cited source of business success *and* business distress by CEOs is relationships. *Period*! Is that a surprise? It shouldn't be. Asked to identify the three biggest challenges he faces as CEO, here is how one CEO put it: "Dealing with people, dealing with people, and dealing with

I know how to build relationships with people. At the end of the day, that is what it is all about.

—Tom Beerntsen
Project Participant

people. I truly believe that is your number-one issue/opportunity. You cannot do it all yourself and you have to build a team; you've got to build a culture."

You do not have to be an extrovert to be good at dealing with relationships. You do need to know how to focus your efforts to promote the quality of relationships you require to function at your best.

The focus of this chapter is on strategies to manage key aspects of relationships that make a big difference in how you implement your duties. However, this discussion presupposes that your foundation of sound business practices related to human resources is already in place. Let's start with a brief review of those elements.

Creating an Ideal Workplace

Take inventory of the status of your own human resources environment as you review the following basic business practices that lay the foundation for good relationships.

Hire Smart

Every CEO I interviewed was emphatic that you must start with surrounding yourself with the best staff: people who are a good fit for you and your organization. As expected, one key aspect of fit is *expertise and skill sets*, with the emphasis on "identifying good people in the areas you don't know much about." That means you will have to guard against being "hesitant to hire very good people because ultimately that will catch up with you." It is far better to have the following attitude: "I would not be CEO today if I did not have enough courage to hire a chief financial officer who I thought was better than I was. Because you cannot move up and take on more responsibility if you do not have somebody behind you to take over what you do."

It is better to have someone with too much fizz than not enough. You can restrain the former; you cannot add fizz to the latter.

—Philip Merrill
Project Participant

The second is *personality* qualities, such as integrity, honesty, and sincerity. Jon Davis, the director of operations for MATRIX Resources, Inc., with the unique perspective of having placed more than two thousand executives prior to becoming one himself, noted that in most cases, when placements did not work out, "It was their work ethic; it was their team workability; it was their communication; it was their demeanor; it was their bedside manner; it was their ethics." Project participant Mary Lou Quinlan, the founder and CEO of Just Ask a Woman, who is "just a big believer in people's inner talents and persona," also declared that she looks for a person who, "as much as anything is someone whose personality and goals are aligned with ours." When looking for a new administrative assistant, she looked for "someone who has great smarts and common sense, and is a good listener," more than a person with prior experience.

If you get the right people, then you're not doing it alone ever.

—Project Participant

To select new hires well you must clarify the most important qualities and skills for yourself and your organization. *Some executives just have a knack for it.* One went so far as to claim, "The only real skill I have is identifying talented people, even in the areas where I don't have expertise." Because of the importance of hiring the best people, some executives prudently enlist their staff who know them and the workings of the organization well.

> I just talked to colleagues, basically, people that I trusted who knew me, and I gave them a quick situation analysis from my perspective. Then they added to it and said, "Yes, and you need somebody who does this, and you need somebody who …"

The bottom line, as Philip Merrill, an American diplomat, publisher, banker, and philanthropist, put it, "You want to hire people you'd tell someone else they would be crazy not to accept."

Foster the Best Work Culture

There are three interrelated aspects of your organization's work culture that have a big impact on reducing distress at the top: staff loyalty, good teamwork, and staff who feel valued.

Loyalty. When your staff is committed to something more than just their paychecks, they are going to be motivated to contribute more and to work through the inevitable hard times in the life of the organization. There are various ways you can promote staff loyalty, each of which reflects your values and those of the company's culture.

My considerable purpose is to lessen people's stress, not increase it. You get a lot more out of people if they are not stressed.
— Philip Merrill
Project Participant

The farsighted executive knows the long-term value of *being considerate* of each individual's goals and general life circumstances. Mary Lou Quinlan saw the hazards of working in a stressful industry. So when she formed her own business, she was determined to create a work environment that is conducive to staff loyalty. "I feel the work my team and I do relies on us feeling as positive and healthy as possible. So it is my job as a leader now to not only manage the natural stress fluxes of work but to guard my team."

For example, she accommodated staff members' need to take time off from work to tend to personal matters such as dealing with children, parents, and purchasing a new home. She did this because she wanted her company to be a place people love to work and would hate to leave.

Some CEOs find that making a *personal connection* with staff can be a good way to foster loyalty. It can be as easy as getting out of your office and mingling with staff in casual ways. "You've got to be out and about and keep your pulse on the company. Stand in line for the sandwiches and be with the troops."

How do you maintain good boundaries while still connecting with and being respectful of people's individual needs? Here is how one CEO described his role.

> You shouldn't get involved in people's personal lives, but knowing that an employee's mother is ninety years old and just moved into a nursing home is very helpful in recognizing what that person is dealing with during that week or during that day, because that might not be the time to turn up the game on them. It may be that you do cut them a bit more slack or you ask them how that's going, or you suggest that they take that Friday off to tend to that.

· · ·

Don't take yourself so seriously. When things go great it's not all because of you. When things go bad, it's not all because of you. Spread the work and the opportunity for support, and you'll go far.

—Jon Davis
Project Participant

· · ·

Another CEO views his company as a four thousand-person team. He promotes a culture where everyone shows *respect and appreciation* for each other as a key ingredient in building staff loyalty. People find it empowering and it makes them want to work there.

Google, widely known for its general philosophy of work, fosters employee loyalty and creativity in its own unique way. "Generous, quirky perks keep employees happy and thinking in unconventional ways, helping Google innovate as it rapidly expands into new lines of business."[10]

· · ·

You can also foster staff loyalty by engaging their deeper values in the service of the company's mission. Dawn Sweeney nicely exemplified this. When I commented on

Communicating the unwavering goal, mission, and objective is important—making absolutely certain people are dedicated and committed to do that—they're not just going through the motions.

—Ron Peltier
Project Participant

· · ·

the fact that it sounded like her staff supported one another well and that they do not get caught up in personal agendas, she talked about keeping the mission of the organization at the forefront. "That is the environment that we've worked very hard to create for our whole team. At the end of the day, we've got a very big mission—to change the quality of life for people as they age, and help them age with grace and dignity—things that really get you out of bed in the morning. In that environment, people are more willing to relinquish ego.

Teamwork. When you encourage and model collaboration, brainstorming, and facilitation of constructive input, it has a synergistic effect in the company. Top-down support for new ideas is basic to a mind-set that fosters teamwork. This includes acceptance of respectful challenges of management's proposals and procedures. Having structures in place that support a team mind-set goes a long way toward creating an optimal work culture. For example, Chris Coile pointed to a weekly collaborative "state of the union" meeting that galvanized his staff,

While detailed guidelines for building a team approach go beyond the scope of this book, a few key observations by project participants will assist you with developing the mind-set that will guide your efforts. Frank Slocumb, district executive of Harris Bank, noted, "My major achievements have come really out of team-based approaches to opportunities. They've been more fun because they've been shared accomplishments, and the amount of activity is higher than it would have been without that."

Chris Coile facilitates the integration of new members into the management team by encouraging them to contribute their own ideas from the start. "What's important is that it's a collaborative effort: showing a lot of respect for them and demonstrating that their opinions are important. I consider it sort of a benign democracy."

As an example of his commitment to the team approach, Chris

. . .

When somebody owns something, they nurture it and work hard to make it successful, meaningful, and enduring.

—Donald Treinen
Project Participant

. . .

described a time when he was trying to convince everyone that a particular marketing strategy was the best. He made a big presentation on the matter and expected everybody to jump onboard. They did not. "They were not crazy about it." Because of his commitment to a work culture that values honesty, he agreed to think about their points. He took their suggestions, modified the program somewhat, and went back to them with the revised plan. His staff knows that if he really believes in a strategy, he is not going to give up trying to convince them. However, if they are all strongly against it, then it is a no go!

Empowerment. An effective way to foster active engagement and productivity in your staff is to make them look and feel good about their contributions. One CEO went so far as to say that you should "make heroes of staff." "Your job is to ensure that your people are successful. The most ineffective managers are the ones who completely take their people for granted or are abusive, because people have no interest at all in those people being successful; in fact, the opposite [is true]."

Those CEOs who have an autocratic style are, as one participant pointed out, often unaware of how self-limiting that can be. "It is a huge inhibitor to the growth of any business. What you do is you develop resentment and rote behavior and a lack of commitment to the highest value and quality—and, the results are lesser."

If you treat everyone around you with respect, you'll be surprised by how much respect you get in return, and that if you lead, they will follow.

—Captain Jeffrey Winter
Project Participant

Once you make empowering staff a priority, it is easy to help them look good. Crucial to your basic management approach is that you treat each staff member with respect and dignity, especially in the way you communicate with them in meetings. Make your praise public and your critical comments private, so that staff members are not berated in front of their colleagues. Be sure they have the tools and strategies they need to operate successfully. Keep your communications open and responsive.

One executive found that adopting a coaching mind-set helps him to show respect to staff and to build their sense of value and effectiveness. This approach, described in the next chapter as a nonheroic leadership model, offers great benefits to you as the leader

I work hard to be both a good manager and leader on the one hand, as well as a good coworker. I don't look at it as my being the boss, but more like being on the team with a little more experience.

—Project Participant

because it frees you up to devote attention to matters only you can handle.

Improving Your People Skills

Raise Your People Quotient (PQ)

Three core factors that play a big part in your ability to foster good work relationships are your *personality style*, especially where you are on the continuum of introversion and extroversion, your *emotional intelligence*, especially your ability to know your own feelings, and your *social skills*, especially your capacity to read social cues. Though often thought of as fixed, these factors are amenable to modification as a function of brain plasticity.[103] I'm not talking of a personality makeover. However, it is nice to know that you can acquire better interpersonal skills by increasing your awareness of key social and emotional factors and by improving your facility with communication.

A good starting place is the following review. As simple and obvious as some of this may seem, I cannot emphasize enough how using this framework can improve your people skills.

Coordinate Your Life with Others

A useful way to understand the interactions between two people is to see it as a *dance,* with each person trying different ways of responding so they both can coordinate their objectives in ways that work well for each.

In your business life, you need to anticipate others' moves and think carefully about your own best moves to achieve your own objectives. Some people approach this process with cynicism and dread, particularly those who have a paucity of good experiences with people. A new perspective is helpful here. When viewed as a dance, the process can be not only positive, but also wholesome, dignified, and minimally distressing—even fun.

For the dance to go well, you need to keep in mind the following principles:

- Part of what drives human relationships is each person's desire to get his or her own needs met.
- Mutual respect and sensitivity to each other's needs allow the relationship to flourish.
- A shared commitment to the ongoing viability of the relationship allows both participants to continue to get their needs met.

When these components are out of alignment, there will be tension or worse.

For example, the troublesome elements of the dance can emerge when one participant's agenda is driven solely by his or her own personal needs. One example is when the other person's goal is to flaunt his or her power, so your input is negated at every step. Another is when you are negotiating with someone who has sidestepped full disclosure, so the process felt uncomfortably disrespectful and deceitful to you.

> If … someone's brilliant work fails again and again as soon as cooperation from others is required, it probably indicates a lack of courtesy—that is, a lack of manners.
>
> —Peter F. Drucker

Viable, long-term relationships do not grow out of such interactions.

Of course, in business as in personal relationships, most people are highly sensitive to feeling that they are being maneuvered into doing something that is not in their best interest. This is often referred to as *manipulation*, and it carries a negative connotation.

However, I want to make a distinction here between maneuvers that are designed to *set up people* in a manner that disregards their needs and interests versus *setting up the elements* that lead to satisfying interactions and equitable outcomes. The former is problematic and likely to be rejected. As long as your focus is the latter, you can take comfort in knowing that manipulating various elements of interactions is something we all do all the time. Then you can be freed up to "manipulate" in the most positive and effective manner.

For example, when you choose to talk with a staff member over a relaxing dinner instead of in your office, are you manipulating? Yes. You are trying to improve the outcome of the conversation by having it in a situation that foster its going better.[104]

Let's assume you are interacting with another person where you are each respectful and considerate of the other, and you both value the relationship (understandably not always safe assumptions!). When the shared agenda is to *coordinate actions*, not each other as people, then the process is less emotionally charged, and the focus can be on the required actions of each for both to benefit

Relationship Mindfulness. A closer look at some key elements of relationships will help you do your part to foster effective ones. Once again, the place to start is *monitoring* the relationship. However, given the complexity of relationships, that can be truly daunting. So what do you monitor? I suggest that the first step in relationship mindfulness is to look at your motives so you can manage them. The ideal is that your dominant objective is to *improve the* relationship, especially its *functionality and satisfaction*. A moment of reflection is often all you need. Just ask yourself, "How will what I am about to do affect our relationship going forward?"

Other people are just mirrors for yourself. So if someone presses your buttons, you should thank that person because he or she is going to set you free.

—Pat Lynch
Project Participant

For example, imagine how different your approach to speaking with someone would be when your main objective is to:

- show the person who is boss,
- build the person's trust in your willingness to explore creative possibilities,
- promote a collaborative alliance,
- groom the person to take on a more challenging role in the organization.

Once aligned with how you hope to influence the relationship, then focus on your specific aims for the interaction, and ask yourself, "What's the point?" Here the objective is on the specific actions you are intending to coordinate.

The clearer you are about these two dimensions the more you can plan your strategy for how to manage the encounter. This is not always as straightforward as it sounds. Sometimes, our own hidden agendas catch up with us. However, if you can be clear about your goals and stay committed to achieving the intended outcome(s), then your steps will be more deliberate and well placed during the *dance*.

Second, you need to monitor the level of *trust* in the relationship. That is based on each person's assessment of how things have gone previously—on the other's sincerity in making promises and their capacity to deliver.

Third, by paying attention to *how you coordinate activities* with each other, you can improve the trust. One of the best ways to accomplish that is to sharpen your communications (hereinafter referring to all forms including spoken, written, electronic, and nonverbal). At the most basic level, the way we coordinate activities is by making requests and promises with one another, and by effectively declining requests of each other.

Relationship Management Skills

Many of the daily interactions that cause distress for executives are those that involve enlisting others' help or declining others' requests. Your success in each of these types of interactions is essential for you to maintain your ongoing composure, satisfaction, and effectiveness.

Learn How to Make Requests. When you are good at making clear and effective requests, you improve your capacity to enlist others. Then you can leverage your effort, which frees you to devote your attention to priorities requiring your specific involvement. It also adds immeasurably to your sense of wellbeing, including feeling more secure because you can count on your ability to get the resources you need from others.

Yet at the very core of many relationship problems is our discomfort with making requests. Whenever you do not seek assistance but you actually need it, you may seem to have saved yourself from interpersonal stress: you don't have to deal with any tension that arises with others whose needs, desires and requests are in conflict with yours. But, it is frequently a bigger and more erosive source of distress, leaving you with too much to do and a likely buildup of resentment toward the important people in your life.

Why do some people have difficulty with requests? There are more reasons than we can consider here, but one myth that gets in the way of requests is the belief that those who care about you should know what you need and offer it—*without your asking!* This myth of the colleague, spouse, or friend as mind reader can leave you feeling hurt and resentful, since your subjective experience may be that the other person didn't "come through for you." And how would that influence future interactions?

You will do best when you approach requests firmly grounded in the knowledge that this is not a test or measure of personal commitment to you. It makes for cleaner, clearer, unencumbered interactions. Your communication is meant to be a *request for action,* one which can be accepted or declined. The other person will respond according to his or her own needs and availability.

Because your relationship as an executive will have an impact on interactions within your company, it is vital that you make clear to the other person when you are making a *request* and when you are issuing a *command.* In this vein, be sure to avoid using an interpersonal pressure tactic, such as guilt or implied threat, based on your role as boss.

You may also find that you can be more comfortable making a request when you can trust the other person to decline. In fact, one effective way to do this is to tell the person that you will only make it if you are convinced that they will be able to decline it. Appendix A provides a template for making requests. Once you gain facility with these guidelines, you will find that making requests comes more easily, and you will be able to ask for what you need while still being sensitive to the basic fabric of the relationship.

Learn How to Decline Requests. Your commitment to working more effectively, feeling less distress, enjoying your life more and being more healthy means you need to get really good at managing requests made of you, including declining them with sensitivity and clarity. It should come as no surprise that the high-level executives interviewed for the CEO Stress Project are good at managing requests.

Under normal circumstances, even when you do not know the person, when someone makes a request of you it activates automatic reactions such as the wish to be nice, good, and to please, as well as the pressure to be obedient. Usually, these reactions are greater when the exchange takes place in person. Furthermore, the meaning of the request for action is invariably embedded in the relationship with the person who is making the request.

If you tend to feel that declining a request is a personal rejection that could jeopardize your relationship, then you are likely to find it very difficult to do. You then become a slave to other people and to your subjective belief about what they want from you. This can easily lead into a dysfunctional pattern of overextending yourself, making unrealistic promises, feeling trapped and resentful, anxious and depressed—and diminished self-respect, and dignity.

Just as when you make a request of someone else, remember that you are responding to the *request* not the person. You can convey that you will not take the particular action that has been requested while still being sensitive to the person and your relationship. (See the guidelines in appendix A.)

Keep in mind that making and declining requests are skills that require practice. You may need to focus on building these skills in accordance with the systematic model for behavior change presented in chapter 3. You may also need to *train* others by explaining your approach to requests and helping them to understand your expectations concerning requests made and received. Be sure to strive for consistency in how you handle making and declining requests so you build mutual trust with and respect for each other

Ease Office Tensions

Two of the more common sources of tension that arise between individuals in the work setting are ambiguity over matters of responsibility for a task; and confusion about the criteria for a job well done. For you to do your part in preventing or resolving these tensions, you need to:

- be precise in your grasp of roles, duties, and functions—your own and others',
- have unambiguous guidelines for what is expected,
- be able to clearly communicate both.

Despite your best efforts, though, there will be times when tensions arise. While it is true some people manage their relationships so well they rarely have major problems, interpersonal tensions do happen in every relationship. The best relationships have reliable self-correcting strategies based on a shared commitment to do what it takes to make the alliance work; when breakdowns do happen, *both* individuals will enter into dialogue to repair and improve their interactions and any damage done to their trust.

At the same time, the project participants made it clear that as a high-level executive it is your responsibility to *lead the way to repairing any tensions.* Whether the tension is small and arises in the context of a single relationship or is large and encompasses a more complex situation, savvy executives know they must own their responsibility as the leader. Honing your people skills includes stepping up to the task of dealing directly with interpersonal tension.

How do experienced executives handle staff tension? Here are some of the approaches they described.

Disarm with Apology. When the source of the tension is small, it is often best to make amends in the moment. This can foster a good relationship and facilitate getting the work done. The objective is to smooth things over in order to facilitate moving forward. Some executives even go as far as apologizing even when they feel that the tension comes primarily from the other person's actions.

Confront when Necessary. Sometimes tension grows out of larger issues or more longstanding patterns. If so, respectful confrontation may be needed to get things back on track. Your commitment to the relationship should be conveyed in the way you approach the other person.

Your reflections in advance of the conversation, or perhaps taking some time to consider the situation with a trusted third party, will help you to vent your feelings and plan an approach before you jump in. Your objective is to maintain the other person's respect and to foster better sensitivity to each other's expectations in future encounters.

Lead Wisely. When the tension is large and complex, smart executives know that sometimes the best thing to do first is to step up and own their responsibility as the leader. The objective is to do what it takes to resolve the tension in a way that fosters the best work alliance, following up later with a more thorough review of the incident and thoughtful resolution. Superintendent of schools Dr. Alan Leis adopts the following mind-set.

I've got to model being the right leader, and the right leader says, "I'm the leader, and I'm responsible, and the buck stops with me." So I've got to take the high road for the sake of the staff and the sake of the board ...

CEO Tom Hood noted that he is especially careful when the source of the tension is that he has made a decision that affects relationships with his staff in an unexpected and unintended manner. "Then we go slow to go fast—you have to backtrack and put energy into the team and relationships to repair them to the point where you can move forward again."

Set Clear Boundaries. You set the stage for clear interactions and productive work relationships when you define the boundaries of your responsibility and availability. Ambiguous, inconsistent, and poorly managed boundaries can easily deteriorate into confusion, pressure, and distress that distract from getting work done and are a drain on energy. Further, by making your boundaries more explicit, you gain the advantage of building them into your company's culture, thus relieving yourself and others of what can otherwise be an ongoing source of pressure.

There are many ways that boundary issues arise, but two common ones include the limits of your availability during the work day and your availability after work.

While you may have a goal of being available to your staff on an as-needed basis, people will certainly have different notions about what warrants your time. Many CEOs find it is necessary to state their policy explicitly for what people can bring to their attention and the type of preparation expected of them. Similarly, you may need to create policies regarding your availability outside the normal workday and your expectations regarding others' availability.

One CEO gave the example of having to train his staff regarding e-mails, particularly his expectations of their replies to those he sent at off-work times.

> Just because I send them a message at 10:00 p.m. doesn't mean I'm looking for an answer that evening. Likewise, I work over the weekend. As I get an idea, where I used to jot a note to myself and then do something about it on Monday, now I send it off to somebody at 6:00 a.m. on a Saturday. And I've had to tell my staff that just because that's the behavior I have, does not mean that's the behavior they must have.

Communicating Better

There are have many opportunities to improve your relationships through how you communicate. This section provides a few key guidelines.

Relational breakdowns can occur as the result of three main communication mishaps:

1. One person's remark is *unintelligible* to another because the words themselves are misheard or not fully understood—you may find you have an employee who consistently seems to get only part of the message, and he then claims no one told him the rest. In speaking with him privately, you discover he has a hearing loss that affects some frequencies that makes it difficult for him to hear certain voices or make fine distinctions between similar words.

2. One person's comment is misconstrued due to a *special meaning* the message has—a new female employee may take umbrage at your asking her to make coffee, thinking it is an example of sexism. What she cannot know is that in your company each employee takes a turn making coffee, men and women alike!

3. The listener's *interpretation* is not consistent with the intended message due to a lack of specificity—your request for support on a new project may be taken as asking for emotional support when you meant that you want the person to pick up the slack on another project.

Each communication breakdown can result in an erosion of basic trust that can erode the fundamental capacity to cooperate, coordinate actions, and harmonize adjustments with one another.

As CEO the most crucial way you can prevent these communication breakdowns is to set standards for communications within your company culture. Be sure to include the expectation that when there is a breakdown both parties are expected to address it ASAP. You will get the best results when you back up explicit policy guidelines with your own modeling. The following template can be modified for your own use.

I want to be sure our interactions go well (explicit positive intent) so I'd like to make an agreement (promoting shared responsibility) that if either of us isn't sure what the other has said that we will be sure to ask for clarification. Though I am the CEO, it is far more important to me that you let me know when you do not understand something I've said then it is that you show deference to me (acknowledging normal discomfort but reframing what is most important). Can you be okay with that that (getting explicit buy-in)?

Once you lay the groundwork for your general approach to communications, there is still some fine tuning to consider.

Go beyond Words

Your words can say all the "right things" yet the outcome can be spoiled by overlooking the impact of the tone of the interactions; the social and relationship context of interactions, and the larger cultural values. Each adds a dimension of meaning to the intended one that can enhance or diminish the impact. It is prudent to be mindful of them.

Body Language. Nonverbal aspects of messages, such as tone of voice, gestures, and facial expression, convey an attitude about the other person and the relationship. As such, they play a big part in how the intended communication is received and interpreted. For example, a critique given to a staff member in a tone of friendly collegiality conveying a desire to be helpful is very different from the same information given with disdain.

Context. This dimension is easy to overlook. A well-intended simple critique from the CEO is likely to have a vastly different meaning than the same one from a colleague.

Likewise, letting your CEO, with whom you have an easy and friendly relationship, know that you are having relationship problems with your life partner could undermine your chances for a promotion. She is likely to be concerned about how your personal turbulence will affect your work. Always remember that she is your CEO, no matter how close and friendly you are.

Consider Personal Meaning

Each person's history gives meaning to events and determines how they see and interpret their experiences. For example, consider the difference in perceptions between Hunter, who has been with the company for just a year and Jon, who has been with the company for five years. Both receive the same news that a major contract has fallen through and this will put the company in a precarious position.

Hunter experienced being let go during the downsizing of his company the year prior to coming onboard. He is much more likely to be alarmed than Jon, who has been through several of these setbacks and has seen how the company rallies to recover and to protect the company and its employees.

Gauge Political Correctness

Popular use of the expression "politically correct" started in the 1970s to describe the use of language that would not cause a person of any demographic group (gender, ethnicity, social or cultural) to feel excluded, offended, or diminished. As our lives become ever more intertwined with people of diverse cultures and backgrounds, the need to be PC is more pertinent.

Political correctness is not just about words, though; it is about accepting and embracing different backgrounds, approaches and ways of thinking. This openness enriches company culture and promotes creativity. Political correctness is an attitude as much as a guideline for language. In the present context, PC refers to the full range of communications and the way we relate to others.

Because building and maintaining good work relations should always be a high priority for you, you must be acutely sensitive to the need for attitudes and behaviors that include, rather than offend, all employees and business contacts. Relationships will be undermined in a company culture that allows for misguided attitudes that convey "my language and my way are right!" The more pervasive the negative attitude, the more it will erode morale within the company.

Sometimes companies must actively seek to learn about other cultures in order to avoid potential misunderstandings. For instance, American companies that have created business alliances in Japan have learned about cultural differences that affect business interactions. Our Western culture places a high value upon qualities such as personal freedom, individualism, and candor, while the Japanese value sharing, cooperation, and respect for authority. Without an appreciation for this difference and some modifications in their approach, Westerners' outspoken and direct style could be misconstrued as a threat to the basic fabric of the business relationship to such an extent that it undermines the negotiations.

Blending Language, Tone, and Context

You can improve the likelihood that an interaction goes well in a subtle yet powerful way by setting the framework for it at the onset. For example, suppose you have received multiple complaints from other staff that Leslie, a senior executive, has been behaving badly, causing staff tensions and disrupting workflow. She has been a valuable staff member for some years who has always had a good relationship within the company. Your objective as CEO is to facilitate her return to her usual standard of excellent performance.

Here is an example of a way to start the conversation that helps *both* of you to approach the meeting in the best frame of mind.

> Hello, Leslie, nice to see you (friendly/collegial tone of voice and gentle smile). Since you are probably wondering why I asked you to meet with me today (empathic statement), let me tell you. As you may know, I've had several people tell me that they are concerned about how things have been going in your department (not: complaints about you), that you've been rather irritable lately and that it's having a bad effect on staff morale. I'm hoping that we can have a conversation (minimizes feelings of being called to the carpet) to see how we can put our heads together (invitation to collaborate) to help the situation improve for all concerned. My objective is to do whatever I can to help your department run better (focus is on work, not personal matters) so the workflow gets back to a better level. So, please help me understand what's been going on from your perspective.

Managing Special Relationships

Throughout the book, I have emphasized that managing work pressures requires both practical and emotional support. Some special supportive relationships must have a higher standard of trust and teamwork than other working relationships—they are vital to your goal of performing at your highest level and staying in your cool zone. They require and deserve your investment of attention, sensitivity and extra effort to make them work.

One CEO was forthright about his no-nonsense utilitarian views of business relationships. He puts them into one of three categories: givers, takers and investors. Accordingly, he goes out of his way to be an investor with others and is looking for people who value their relationship with him and are invested in it.

This strategy underscores the reality that you need to be as judicious about your efforts in relationships as you are in financial investments. You cannot afford to get bogged down in relationships that drain your resources. Successful CEOs learn how to manage this dimension in politically correct ways.

Administrative Assistants

Many of the CEOs stated that they are not good with details; some are not good at organizing materials and planning. In order to be effective in their work and free from distress, they must trust that these matters are managed well. The solution is that they wisely decide *not* to put their efforts into developing these skills beyond a rudimentary level. Instead, they hire a high-caliber administrative assistant (AA) with whom they build a powerful alliance.

The AA must be attuned to your best interests including your personal preferences, sensitivities, as well as those things that are of very little interest or concern to you. At the same time, the AA must train you to manage details in the ways the AA requires to do his or her job.

For this level of synchronization to become operational and to remain so, it takes concerted *effort* by both participants, especially in the early stages of their relationship. Their initial effort focuses on building teamwork. They handle ongoing maintenance by open dialogue and as-needed meetings. Some prefer routine structured meetings.

Some CEOs also have a separate executive assistant with whom they collaborate on how to handle issues as well as to decide which of them will be the representative at each meeting. Some executives collaborate with a specialized team.

I share what I'm dealing with and going to do with a small group of people that are my trusted team. I want their opinions, but they know at the end of the day, I'll make a decision one way or the other.

Some CEOs also have personal assistants to pick up some of the nonwork details of their lives so that they can devote their attention to work matters.

Confidants

Most high-level executives find it is prudent to have emotional support for the tough times, even though it is more natural for some than others to seek that support for their work.

Mary Lou Quinlan, who has written[105] about the emotional support required to sustain the rigors of corporate life, described both the need for and the ambivalence often associated with emotional support. "There is something about the crusade to the top that you feel you have to be like Mighty Mouse, saving the day all the time. You need to know that you are not alone, that there are people you can share concerns with along the way. It is positive, helpful; you learn, you grow, as opposed to feeling you're diminished in any way."

She also spoke specifically about the role that a beloved spouse or personal partner can play in helping executives to maintain perspective. "I believe with all my heart that you must have someone in your life who loves you just the way you are. I think that's really important, because you are going to put these standards on yourself to go higher and higher. There has to be somebody who reflects back to you: 'You are perfect now, the way you are, if nothing else happens.'"

It is in the context of this personal relationship that one can vent candidly about the day's challenges.

What helps you to get past things at work and then not bring them back or rehash them is to share them with your spouse, and just sort of get it off your chest. Especially when you've been married a while, you know that your spouse loves you and respects you, so you can just go ahead and blurt out everything, vent basically, get it done. It's about getting it out of your system and being able to move on. That should be part of what a partner or a friend is.

Alan Leis noted that at times, it can be immensely helpful just to have a relaxed reflective conversation with a best friend or life partner. "So, usually what I do is—if it has been a particularly interesting, difficult, or stressful day—sit back and have a glass of wine and talk with my wife about the day, just so she can serve as a sounding board."

One CEO noted the value of a fresh perspective, such as "talking to friends who have no clue about my actual business. Their insight into it can be very valuable because they have no political leaning. They don't know the players; they don't know the business."

Still, as Bob Castle, MS, SPHR, senior director of Human Resources at Woodbourne Center, Inc., pointed out, sometimes it is a confidant within the organization who offers just the right combination of emotional support and expertise.

When I have messed up, I go to Stan and I say, "Stan, I need help." He will gently help untangle things yet still keep in touch with the reality. "Okay, we've made some mistakes here. We've got to put ourselves in a recovery mode. Let's be realistic about it, but also be kind to yourself about it."

With such important contributions to your quality of life and work performance, it just makes sense to invest some time and attention to your supportive relationships. Nonetheless, there is a tendency in executive circles to think of the time spent on nurturing supportive relationships as time taken away from important work. If you think of these relationships, instead, as essential to the synergy that allows you to perform at a high level and to live your best life, then you will find ways to give them their due.

If your life is light on supportive relationships, you may need to be more deliberate about setting up what you need. The buddy system, first described in chapter 4, applies here.

The Buddy System

The pressure to stay cool in the executive hot seat permeates your daily life as a CEO. Prudent CEOs respect the strain and risk that this pressure places them under, so they develop a buddy system. As you learned earlier in the book, the buddy system is modeled after military and scuba diving models; it is a partnership built upon the principle of zero tolerance for error in order to maximize safety and performance. It ensures an interdependent system of two people looking out for each other.

There are many possible choices for buddies. You can look within your work circle, such as a senior executive or your AA. Or you may prefer someone from outside your own company, perhaps another CEO, your spouse, or a friend. Your choice of who you want to enlist as a buddy may be dictated, in part, by your specific objectives. It is common, for example, for individuals to enlist a family member if the goal is to increase your ability to let go of work concerns and to be fully present when you get home. A work colleague would be a good choice if your goal is to improve your ability to maintain your cool when department meetings become challenging. In both cases, you would give your buddy the authority to alert you when you are going off course.

For a buddy system to be effective, several key ingredients are required.

Selectively Reveal Weakness. For buddies to help one another, they must know what weak spots to look out for. This can be difficult for those who subscribe to the belief that a CEO should not reveal vulnerability or weakness. Savvy executives recognize the value of having someone watch their back. When and what you share is dictated by your goals and by your own comfort level. Of course, like any relationship, when things go well, one's trust and comfort grows over time.

Develop Healthy Interdependence. *Inter*dependence is quite different from dependence, which is a state of one person carrying the heavy load. Interdependence means that you each rely on the other to provide what you need to perform at your best. The buddy system is fully intended to enhance autonomous functioning, but you help each other to do so.

Clearly Define Objectives. You and your buddy must be clear about when you are to be alerted that you are straying off course. Possible red flags might be when you are coming on too strong with clients when you are getting irritable with staff members, when you are losing your focus on a project, when you are showing signs of fatigue or when you are neglecting a personal relationship. Your buddy's objectives may be different.

Like every important relationship, the buddy system is a dynamic one that needs ongoing attention to keep it working well. Periodically check with your buddy for their input. Make sure to nourish the relationship by providing praise, explicitly expressing the value of a particular way that your buddy is helping you.

Corporate Peers

Some CEOs seek educational and emotional support from local chapters of national organizations, such as the Young Presidents Organization, Vistage, Society of International Business Fellows, Inner Circle, and TEC. They offer educational workshops that focus on special issues pertaining to business, as well as individual and group consultations.

Some of the organizations also provide meetings that focus on personal issues, such as family, kids, and life. "It opens a door to everybody's lives, and you can watch lots of people in the same position and see how their cards are played out in advance." One of the younger CEOs noted that he especially values being with a "more seasoned group of executives. I appreciate surrounding myself with people who have already seen the movie, or have been in the pitfalls I am headed for."

Some CEOs prefer to organize their own peer support, such as regularly scheduled working lunches. Here is how Carolyn B. Elman reflected on the value of her own peer circle.

> You bring up an issue to the group and talk through it, or listen to somebody else's issues. It is so easy to see it when it's somebody else's issue. Then you take some of that back to your own workplace and say, "Hmm, that's exactly what we were talking about." And over time, you develop friendships with them.

David Nour, MBA, founder and managing partner, The Nour Group, Inc., who exuded an especially strong, take-charge approach to his business, got tired of feeling frustrated by "confusing *vibration with forward motion!*" Recognizing the need for an *independent audit or perspective* so he could get better ROI, he started asking peers who knew him well for input. Over a period of five years, he built a personal board of advisors.

> We visit once a quarter over dinner. What I greatly appreciate is that they say, "David, knowing you, that's a great idea, go for it," or, "David, knowing you, what the hell are you thinking? That's probably not a good place for you to invest time, effort, and resources."

Specialized Consultants

When you are intent on being a shrewd CEO and sustaining optimal functioning over the long haul, you must essentially leave your narcissistic needs with the security guard as you enter the company facilities. Then you can be free to seek the best guidance you can get when you really need it. In fact, CEOs who consistently perform at their best have a team of experts they call upon as needed.

Unfortunately, acceptance of the need for consultation too often comes only when desperation sets in. For example, reflecting on the way things were before he enlisted a coach, one CEO noted that his marriage ended in divorce because, "I did everything myself. I was working seven days a week and my wife couldn't take it anymore." He eventually used a coach to develop work practices *and* ways of caring for his personal needs.

The function of the consultant can be whatever you believe would improve your functioning and satisfaction, including assisting you with sorting out which kind(s) of expert to enlist. Think of the variety of trainers and coaches top athletes use. There are business consultants and coaches who focus on conventional business matters such as business plans, leadership, organization and team building, and program development, as well as those who focus on integrating work and personal life. When the frustrations you encounter recur and seem intractable, then you may benefit from psychotherapy.

Make It Happen

Step One. What aspect of relationship management stands out to you as a target area for improving your executive performance? Consider your performance in relation to the broad areas presented in the chapter: creating an ideal workplace, people skills, managing office tensions, communication, and managing special relationships. Choose the area that deserves some special effort on your part in order to improve your overall performance and reduce distress.

Step Two. Now, narrow your focus within the category and select one specific aspect to focus on. As I have emphasized throughout, you are more likely to follow through and to succeed if you choose a meaningful goal and are realistic about improving in a stepwise fashion.

Step Three. Formulate an action plan using the Action Plan Template in chapter 3. Keep in mind that it is very important that you succeed, because part of what you are learning is how to make meaningful changes. Then you can take on more challenging matters later on. In that regard, one key component of success is creating a path that is specific, realistic, and sustainable.

Chapter 13

MANAGING WORKFLOW

*I have found consistently absent in the individuals who are failing
the ability to make good assessments of their situations,
to develop plans that really make sense,
and to take actions that have good outcomes
over long periods of time.*

—Richard R. Kilburg

The pressure to manage your daily workflow and to accomplish your goals requires you to bring together all the skills you have learned so far to help you remain cool in the executive hot seat

Anxiety is caused by a lack of control, organization, preparation, and action.

—David Kekich

You know from your experience that each day brings you face to face with the demands of many immediate tasks, longer-term projects, and management of related interpersonal challenges. All this must happen in the context of long-range planning for the company—foreseeing where the company needs to go and what it will take to get there.

This is where you as a CEO live each moment of the workday. It is where you need to be as composed and in command as possible—and often when alone and in the face of pressures from many different people.

You must be able to focus on what is crucial and be decisive in how to allocate your own and the company's resources.

What is it going to take to pull this off? Throughout this book, you have learned skills to master these challenges in ways that create synergy and bring success and satisfaction to your life. You learned to create the ideal executive performance state by utilizing the Hardiness for Hard Times mind-set, the Personal Positioning System (PPS), and the self-care methods described in earlier chapters.

While there are many valuable books on business management and leadership,[106] I have taken a different perspective in this book and focused on your individual and personal ways of engaging the challenges. Now let's apply all that you have learned to the very practical issues of how you perceive your daily work, your role in managing it, and the methods that enable you to be systematic and strong in your execution.

On a daily basis, the objective is for you to:

- be confident that what you are doing is congruent with your role, your responsibilities, and your personal values,
- be engaged in the work in a meaningful and satisfying way,
- be confident that you *are doing* what you need to be doing at any given time,
- trust that it's all right to be *not doing* what you're not doing at any given time,
- minimize distress.

Overseeing the Overwhelming

Your Leadership Mind-set

The general mind-set you bring to the role of CEO is the primary filter through which you perceive your tasks and dictates how you formulate strategies for dealing with them. Mind-set is the scaffolding on which you hang your notions of how you should operate, yet it generally remains in the background, outside of your awareness. For you to gain and sustain the capacity to be cool while facing your daily challenges, you must be certain that your mind-set is taking you in the right direction

Even though there have been some shifts over the past several years, there still exists in many circles a cultural pressure to be a heroic leader. A heroic leader uses his or her authority to make unilateral decisions and carries the company forward using muscular strength that minimizes the input of others. It can be an intoxicating position; however, as explained by Michael Hopkins[107] in an insightful article, the pressure to be a charismatic leader is a powerful prescription for distress, because you are "counted on to be tireless, indomitable, never out of answers." This can create a large mental trap, fostering feelings of being overly responsible.

185

Hopkins advocates, instead, for an *antiheroic* leadership model. The antiheroic leader is one who focuses on a collaborative model that builds on the strength of individuals and teams. It is still a position of authority, but this mind-set leads to a different approach than that of the heroic leader. For example, the heroic leader might approach an idea for a project by asking, "How am I going to do that?" The antiheroic leader would ask, instead, "Who can do that?" "Who knows how to do that?" "Who can help me get that done?"

As one seasoned CEO noted, your role for any given project is then determined by first assessing project goals, who should be involved and why. "Then, with that kind of a framework, I can answer the question, what is my role?" Another CEO noted this often means, "You end up working with your senior team to guide them on the implementation."

The nonheroic model has its own challenges and may require some adjustment. Of particular note, you have to relinquish doing things yourself and getting them done 100 percent your way. This, despite the fact that in other phases of your career, directly managing tasks and projects, taking initiative, and being industrious probably worked quite well for you.

Shifting your style may require you to give up doing things by instinct, to realize that you cannot do it all, to forego the illusion of being in control, and to learn how to get things done through other people. Reflecting on such a transition, CEO and president Mike Pappas noted, "Up until five years ago, I was spinning the hats—dealing with the people and the daily grind. Now it's trying to clarify that process into structure and trying to hire the right people to do it through them."

Years ago, I had a client who was stuck in this transition. A brilliant visionary with a strong entrepreneurial spirit, he had started a business and grew it to a multimillion-dollar enterprise. Nevertheless, he lacked the skills for delegating and working collaboratively with his staff. The sad result was that he became enormously frustrated and angry, because he could not implement his ideas. His irritability eroded both his staff and personal relationships.

The shift to the nonheroic leadership model not only results in reduced pressure, but also a new type of gratification that comes from coaching others. Of course, there are some mind traps to watch for here, too. Lookout out for being either too eager to assign work to others, or reluctant to let go of things you enjoy doing even when there are more important places to put your energy.

Your Priorities

In addition to mind-set, a second major factor that determines how you manage workflow is your priorities. You had an opportunity to consider the core values that direct your personal life in chapter 2: Setting Your Sails for Success. Now, we consider the values that guide successful CEOs as they set their business priorities on a daily basis. Here are several guideposts that stood out from the interviews.

Staying True to Company Values. Successful executives manage work tasks based on a clear grasp of company values, and their responsibility for dealing with them. Adherence to these priorities provides the lens through which they continually evaluate tasks and determine the nature of their duty in any dealings with them. Unclear and weakly held values leave you vulnerable to distractions, especially to the agendas of others, and may lead into turmoil that saps your energy. By the time you are aware of the problem, you may have unwittingly created complications and expended a lot of energy.

Being Prepared. All the CEOs I interviewed insist on being well prepared to face the demands of their work. Feeling unprepared is dreaded. These are people of their word. "Whenever you say you're going to do something, deliver." One of their biggest sources of distress is when their preparation is tied to the performance of someone who does not do their part.

Getting a High Return on Investment (ROI). Successful CEOs seek ways to get value out of everything they do. "It doesn't mean you have to be work-productive in the usual sense every minute of the day. But it is seeing the value of what you are doing, including resting." They look for ways to leverage their efforts, such as using hidden pockets of time in productive ways. For example, one CEO handled his frustration with the large amount of time he spent traveling to meetings and events by making the time more productive. He began inviting a staff member to go with him so they could converse in transit. "I find doing this not only valuable business-wise, but I find it valuable in that I'm finding ways to find value in everything I'm doing."

Do it Now. Make it Happen. By and large, the interviewees are "get it done" sort of people. They place a high value on completing tasks quickly, efficiently, and effectively. In-tolerant of being bogged down with accumulated, leftover tasks, they seek expediency. They spend little time ruminating, instead concentrating on going from reflection to action. The mind-set that Chip Schunemen, MBA, president at Kaplan IT Learning, Inc., uses is

> Do what you can, do it right, do it now, and learn to let go. By doing it now, you are recognizing that in the next ten minutes, or the next hour, or the next day, there are going to be a whole slew of other issues that are going to come up. So you need to take care of it now. Otherwise, you're just going to end up in an overwhelming situation.

Staying True to Oneself. Successful CEOs remain cool by integrating their core values and self-wisdom into the mind-set and strategies they bring to the work. They engage the work meaningfully and with minimal distress by staying aligned with their character, strengths, and weaknesses, their needs, values, beliefs, and career mission.

Streamlining Workflow

Organize

The vital importance of being well organized warrants mention here. When you know where your "stuff" is and have easy access to it, you can focus fully on the content, rather than the mechanics, of your work. Think of the surgeon who knows where each instrument is and knows who will assist him at each moment.

> *We need to constantly define and redefine what we are trying to accomplish on many different levels, and consistently reallocate resources toward getting these tasks completed as effectively and efficiently as possible.*
>
> —David Allen

Keeping track of all the stuff of your work can truly be daunting. Furthermore, you should expect that as your career and business evolve, and the volume and complexity of what you are responsible for increases, you will need to improve how you manage details. Weaknesses in your system undermine your capacity to be in synch with the real elements that foster success—leadership and managing people and projects. Disorganization causes distress. Surely, it undermines feeling cool![108]

Plan

You know the essential role of planning in staying in touch with your priorities and achieving goals. Yet, one of the great challenges you face as CEO is to do the work of planning! That means *making* the time for it. You must pull yourself out of the river's current, and step back to see how the flow of the river fits into the broader landscape.

Regardless, it is common for CEOs to neglect making time for planning because of several competing factors. One is the pressure to move quickly into action, including getting caught up with meetings and what other people need from them, only to end the day or week with their own priorities left unattended

> *What you're managing is doing the work in a way that is going to produce the right results, rather than swinging madly like a boxer in distress.*
>
> —Ed Kelley
> Project Participant

Another is the discomfort that naturally arises while planning. Though you might expect to feel calmer and more in control when you can see the larger picture, unfortunately that is not always the case. When you first begin to consider the broader perspective you may see some things that are troubling, such as elements that need attention and places where the company or your leadership are coming up short. Although systematic enquiry is the rational next step, it is human nature to want to turn away from the challenging task. So it is *essential* you create routines that build review and enquiry into your ongoing schedule.

It will also help if you, or your assistant or buddy, remembers that any short-term discomfort is an investment in your ability to have peace of mind. The more you feel that you are on secure footing with the larger picture, the easier it is to tolerate the ongoing sources of distress.

Plan Short-Term. To assure that the planning takes place, successful CEOs develop and faithfully use a variety of methods (often rituals). The variability is testimony to the axiom that there is no right way to plan. Rather, you have to develop a method that works for you and is sufficiently flexible to absorb changes. A common practice to make planning go well is to develop a template to review the many tasks, goals, deadlines, and other matters that come up routinely.

Consider your current planning methods. Are they really sufficient? The Weekly Focusing Questions in figure 13.1 can serve as a template for your review. Modify it as needed, and regularly reassess your planning methods to determine if they need to be revised to meet current demands.

The timing and methods for planning used by successful CEOs range from minimally structured to highly organized and systematic. Planning may take place on a daily or a weekly basis, at the start or end of the day and/or week, and sometimes even on the weekend. A few do their planning on the road, on the way to or from work. Some do their planning on their own, but many meet with their administrative assistant to co-create the plan. And a few delegate the responsibility for daily planning almost exclusively to their AA. What is essential is that you engage the task fully and that you regularly evaluate how well your method is working.

Weekly Focusing Questions

What specific questions do you need to ask yourself that allow you to filter the tasks?

Which of the questions need to be asked each day, week, every two weeks, or once a month?

What do you need to look at? Which tickler file systems do you need to check and when?

How often do you need to look at certain tasks and areas of responsibility to ensure that everything works as a consistent system, freeing you to think and manage at a higher level?

Which areas are you micromanaging? Which tasks should be delegated? To whom? When? What would it take to make this happen? How will this benefit you? How will it benefit the Project?

Which tasks need to be monitored each day? On a certain day? At a designated time?

What improvements do you need to make in your weekly and daily plans to improve productivity and to free you from distress?

How are your relationships with Company staff and clients going? Which ones need special attention this week?

How can you improve communications with staff and clients? How can you improve guidelines for when they seek your input?

How can you make the weekly planning and reviewing sessions function better? Is the schedule working? Do you need better ways to protect your time and privacy?

What routines and policies could you develop for yourself and your staff that would make the workflow and staff relations go better?

How would you benefit from consulting with team members, other senior executives, administrative assistants, and the board of directors on how things are going? What would it take for you to enlist their support?

What additional questions do you need to ask yourself each week?

Figure 13.1

Plan Long-Term. Planning for bigger projects often takes place at dedicated meetings, such as company retreats or in weekly, quarterly, and annual meetings. Successful CEOs have systematic ways of keeping these larger goals in the front of their minds. For example, one keeps the company goals in a little bound notebook he takes with him everywhere. That way he can glance at it periodically to make sure his efforts are in line with his larger goals. He monitors and revises his shorter-term plans accordingly throughout the week.

Set Priorities. A full discussion of specific business methods for setting priorities goes beyond the focus of this book. Our focus here is on the psychological strategies for prioritizing. Use the following guidelines, delineated by Pat Troy, CAE, founder and president, FacetsWoman, Inc., to get the best results from your efforts.

> Plan so that you have a strategy, you know where you're going and you can measure along the way. Then try to live in the moment, but check off things as you go. In other words, define in advance what many of those moments should be, focus on them, and don't bite off more than you can chew.

Build in Breathing Room. You must value the quality of your experience during the workday, or surely, the work will dominate you. Build in wiggle room. Make sure you have a "user-friendly" schedule, with free time built into each day to absorb the inevitable unexpected things that arise.

That may seem like a tough recommendation, because your likely inclination is to cram as much as you can into your day. Nevertheless, as you pay better attention to the "stress messenger," you will realize how frequently you feel crunched. So, the prudent approach is to reframe the "extra" time from a luxury to a *necessity.*

You can set up buffer zones by blocking out specific times that no one is able to schedule for you. Then use the time to plan, debrief between meetings, or just take a break.

There's just not enough time. In an ideal world, you would have infinite time to spend on each thing. But you don't.

—Project Participant

· · ·

Any one day I will know exactly what I am doing the next day and the day after within reason. But the most important thing is, I don't plan the day to be such that I can't cope with the unexpected.

—Clinton Wingrove
Project Participant

· · ·

There are several variants on the buffer zone strategy. You can set up arbitrary rules to protect the time. For example, one CEO does not agree to meetings that start after 4:00 p.m. She knows that she does not function well at that time of day, and that she wants to get home to be with her family. The buffer zone gives her "a float moment to pack my stuff up and get my head together." Another CEO noted that he gives himself a break from the routines by working from home one day out of every two weeks.

Designate Specific Times. The main purpose for planning is to be confident throughout the day that you know what you must accomplish and that you have a reliable way to make it happen. To do so, you must designate specific times during the day for the precise tasks that must get done. Period. You must put yourself in charge of your time and create the dedicated work sessions you need to complete your high-priority tasks, even as other pressures threaten to undermine your good intentions. Being in charge in this way helps you stay cool and composed throughout the day and enables you to let go of work at the end of the day.

Even with the best of intentions, it is difficult to assess accurately the time needed for some tasks. Particularly when you are planning your work time for a new or unfamiliar task, your estimate of how much time it will take is likely to be off. Some people find it helpful to handle this by estimating the time required and then doubling or tripling it.

An example of the Hardiness For Hard Times approach is to incorporate a time study into your plan. How long do you think the task will take? Do an estimate before starting the work, and then time the activity to see how much time it really takes. This simple strategy has two valuable benefits: it gives you hard data that you can use the next time you do the task and monitoring the actual time while performing the task will keep you incentivized to work efficiently.

Formulate a Job Well Done. Once you have completed your plan for the day, filter it through the following two questions and revise accordingly.

When I look back on the day as I depart from the office, what will I see that will make me feel rock solid and proud about how I managed my time? What do I need to accomplish today, and how do I need to handle the day, so when it's time to go to sleep tonight I can have peace of mind?

Expect Uncertainty. Of course, there are always elements over which you have no control. Factors outside of the company, as well as inside your own business, can affect you in large and small ways.

Successful CEOs manage uncertainty by both broadening their focus and then narrowing it, in turn. They try to avoid nasty surprises in the larger sense by staying informed of the range of factors influencing their business. They routinely scan trade journals, follow the news carefully, and investigate relevant issues more deeply. However, they also learn strategies to reduce their concerns about troubling matters that remain, like this one Bob Castle uses.

> I force myself to think about the worst-case scenario and how I would deal with it. I ask systematically, "What are the odds of this or that happening?" I identify where I need to put my efforts. "Where are my high leverage points right now?" I need to let go of the fact that I can get blindsided, because I can't deal with that. You can't control conditions or other people. But, you can control yourself. So you must focus on what you can deal with and don't get distracted by all of the stray bullets that are flying around.

Track Priorities

To have peace of mind about what you are doing, as well as what you are not doing, you must have methods for monitoring workflow. These range from simple checklists to comprehensive software programs.

> Most days, I don't accomplish anywhere near everything I would like to, but it's important to prioritize. It's constant reassessing priorities.
>
> —Pat Troy
> Project Participant

The Personal Positioning System, presented in chapter 2, provides a general model for overseeing workflow. It can easily be adapted to use as a tool to monitor your status on tasks and projects. With regular use, you can stay on top of the progress made, resource allocation, and actual use (staff, time, budget) as well as your own personal resources.

At the practical level, some CEOs rely solely on digital technology. Many others find that a mix of paper and digital devices works best. For some CEOs, the act of putting pen to paper is part of the process of planning. CEO Mike Pappas noted, "Writing things down is helpful because it forces me to get my thoughts clear about where I'm going and where I'm trying to end up." Many CEOs carry a small bound booklet to jot things down in the middle of meetings and conversations. For them, it is easier then entering information into an electronic device, and it reduces the risk of losing information. It is useful as a way of keeping goals and agendas in view to buffer against the many pressures of the day, and is a concrete record that can be used for review and planning. Of course, all these same tasks can be accomplished through digital technology as well.

Then there are the CEOs, like Dawn Sweeney, who rely more upon their *internal navigation systems*.

> I set my priorities up for the quarter and then I never look at them again, because I totally internalize them. I can't necessarily just reel them off like I've memorized them. It's more that I've got them like at a cellular level. I know what they are, so I go through this process in my own mind of just remapping my priorities.

In keeping with the Hardiness for Hard Times approach, it is important that you regularly evaluate your tracking methods and look for ways to modify your strategies to make them easier, more automatic, and more reliable.

Handling Disruptions

Be Flexible and Persistent. In response to the many potential disruptions that can occur over the course of a day, when do you persist with your intended task and when do you flex your schedule? Of course, this is not really an either/or question. In fact, in order to manage workflow well, you must find creative ways to do both.

> A lot of people give in too quickly when they run into a road block rather than trying to find an alternative way to make their plan work. The thing is, there are so many creative solutions to almost anything. It's important just to push through, and not abandon the idea, the concept, or the time frame that you're

trying to get. That is predicated on a strong sense of what you're trying to pull off.

Running a business is analogous to climbing a mountain. Because it is so clear that you cannot defeat the mountain, you must be flexible in adapting to its demands while moving toward your goals. If you don't modify your pace or path as conditions change, the mountain will defeat you. Yet, at the same time, you must persist toward your goal. For some CEOs, the nature of their work demands that they plan on frequent disruptions. So how do they combine flexibility with persistence? Here is how Don Treinen does it.

I go into each day with a mind-set of what I know is likely to change, and am prepared for that by keeping track of those things that I had to put on the side burner. Throughout the day, I pause to see how things are unfolding.

Regain Your Focus. While disruptions can interfere with the flow of your mental and emotional energy, you can learn methods to manage disruptions and foster the ability to regain your ideal executive performance state. "When I can reorient myself and stay focused … on the objectives that I set out to accomplish in the short-term, the intermediate term, and the long-term, I really spend zero time worrying."

All you can do is be in charge of the moment by doing what you need to do using your skills, ability and wisdom.

—Clarke Langrall Jr.
Project Participant

In response to any disruption, you have three options: dispense with it right away, delegate it, or defer it. This may involve shifting away from a focus on completely resolving the matter to ask instead, "What is the best next step needed to move this issue forward?"

It is not always easy to maintain your presence of mind when others are looking to pass along their sense of urgency. In chapter 12: Relationship Management, you learned about setting clear boundaries. Here is where that work pays off. The more decisive and firm you are, the more comfortable you will be with managing these situations and the more likely you are to gain others' compliance. Your manner and tone of voice will have a big impact on the response you get.

Use the following guidelines when you consider how to respond to a disruption.

1. *Consider the Context.* What are the available options for what you can do in the immediate situation? Do you have the resources (schedule, project, or contract information) you need to deal with it?

2. *Clarify Expectations.* Is the request something you should be dealing with? If yes, what part of it? Seek to clarify responsibilities. For example, you might explain that in the future you expect the person to attempt to solve the problem through other channels, and/or to be clearer about what specifically he needs from you before seeking your input.

3. *Respect the Relationship.* Consider how your response (the tone, content, and your decision) will affect the relationship you have and/or are developing. Sometimes, the relationship factor takes precedence over others, because the outcome will have lasting impact on future interactions. You might want to go out of your way if the relationship is still in building mode, so you can establish the trust you need to cement the foundation.

4. *Think about Time.* How much time do you have to devote to the matter right now? The more thoroughly you have planned your priorities for the day, the easier it will be to assess this.

5. *Examine Your Energy.* Do you have the physical and emotional energy to deal with the issue? Your decision should be based on the priorities you have set for yourself and a realistic appraisal of your energy stores for successfully meeting the remaining demands of the day. For example, if it has already been an especially demanding day and you have a key meeting in an hour, you may need to take a break to recover your energy and to plan for the meeting. Or perhaps it is near the end of the day and you have an important family function to get to. You may need to ensure that you are not depleted when you leave the office.

6. *Pay Attention to Priorities.* How important is this issue and how does that compare to the other priorities that you have set for yourself? Your answer will help to determine whether you should be tenacious in sticking with your plan or whether flexibility is

called for. For example, if one of your personnel management goals is that you want the person now making a request to seek your input more, you might put more weight on responding in an encouraging manner than you would otherwise.

Managing Your Inbox

By far one of the more troublesome aspects of the contemporary work environment is the streaming flow of communications. Voice mail, email, and text messages keep you connected, but also interfere with your focus. Each ping, like a knock on your door, signals someone wants something from you. Because you are a social being, you are likely to be more reactive to these pressures than, say, a paper document that can be left unopened or easily put in a file. This, then, is another situation that requires the effective use of brain guards to diminish the chaos, limit disruptions, and manage your work efficiently.

Install Guardrails, Not Barriers. There is a simple and effective way to guard against electronic intrusions: just turn off all electronic devices when it is time to do focused work. However, that is only the first part of the solution. By all means, close the door to your office and get to work. Only turn on the devices when your work session is complete. That is a way to insure that nobody can disrupt you, and it eliminates the temptation to check for messages or search online.

Nevertheless, that solution is too simplistic. It may well leave you with a realistic worry about losing access to others. That worry will cause its own internal distraction. While it is important to create protective guards against disruptions, you cannot let these become barriers to important communications.

Coordinate with the key people in your network to set up systems and guidelines for when you need to be alerted, despite your plan for focused and uninterrupted work time. By putting some advance effort into creating systems for yourself and doing it in a collaborative manner with associates and staff, you will improve your work environment *and* your alliance with them. The peace of mind thus achieved further enhances your capacity to immerse your mind in the work at hand.

Designate a Message-checking Time. In most cases, it is counterproductive to check messages throughout the day. Generally, it is more productive to set up designated times for checking messages, such as two to four times a day. No more. Reserve one of those times to respond to messages. The objective should be that your schedule allows for good coverage of communications from others *and* that it preserves and protects your designated work periods. If it is not a designated time to check, keep the e-mail program closed and the alert signals on your phone turned off.

When you catch yourself checking more often, ask yourself if it is really necessary. Sometimes, our own anxiety keeps us from focusing on our priorities. So, when you notice that you are slipping into constant monitoring of the digital stream, consider the following questions. "Could it be that I am having difficulty with the work I am supposed to be doing? Is there some-thing else that is making me anxious?" If the answer to either of these questions is affirmative, use the nine-step stress reduction method described in chapter 5 to manage your concerns more effectively.

Install Filters. Make the process of checking messages more efficient by setting up "filters," such as

- separate mailboxes for messages from the most important senders that you check on a priority basis
- subject line filters to ease screening of messages. Be sure to identify key words you and your staff will use.
- standards for length of messages and number of topics included in a single message to keep e-mails manageable

Here is an example of how one CEO manages her e-mail messages in the context of her priorities.

When I know what the biggest priorities of the week are, I perform triage on the 150 e-mails I get a day. I do it by saying, "I need to look at those now, because it is either urgent ... or it is related to the three most important things I'm trying to do this week." Then I take the others and put them into a category where I will look at them if I'm able to.

Jon Davis, who works in a very e-mail-intense environment, developed a strategy for dealing with e-mail that meant changing his mind-set of "living by e-mail." In addition to blocking out times to check for messages, he enlisted an assistant to screen them.

I empowered her to make a lot of those almost rote decisions herself. She responds with some stock responses, and funnels to me the ones she is unsure about or that she feels need to come directly from me.

As one of the early leaders of the electronic workplace, Bill Gates[109] was well aware of the problem of information overload, as well as the risk of information *underload.* "Being flooded with information doesn't mean we have the right information or that we're in touch with the right people." The challenge, as he further explained, "isn't how to communicate effectively with e-mail, it's ensuring you spend your time on the e-mail that matters most." Gates and his staff developed a filtering system. He received a maximum of one hundred e-mail messages a day, plus a summary of important content from other e-mails based on staff review.

Like Gates, it is important to remember that it is your key principles and priorities that help you accept the limits of how much information you can process. By default, successful business executives must learn to let go of the rest.

Coordinate with Key Contacts. When first implementing guidelines to protect your time and manage your own limited resources, it is essential that you coordinate your new policies with your staff. You may find some initial resistance to the higher expectations on your staff to filter their own and others' demands for your immediate input. Explain the value of the changes and provide clear guidelines.

Taking Stock and Moving On

At the end of the workday, most people find themselves reviewing and evaluating their efforts and their accomplishments. Your findings will determine how you feel about your performance and how well you can let go of the day. To do an honest evaluation, you need both objective and subjective criteria. This offsets any tendency to be unrealistic in your expectations of what you could have done on this day, as well as any unrealistic goals of the organization.

Your objective criteria are important, because they will be a marker of your productivity. How did you do on the priorities you set for yourself?

However your subjective criteria are equally crucial if your goal is to be at peace with yourself. Are you satisfied with your accomplishments? Are you proud of how you managed yourself and the workflow on this day? If not, it is important that you arrive at a meaningful understanding of what went wrong. For example, perhaps you failed to appreciate in advance some situational factors that would influence your day. Or perhaps you overestimated your capacity to complete a task.

· · ·

In the end, what you did is what matters. When you think about something, that's a dream; and when you envision doing it, that's a plan. But when you put it on your calendar and then do it, that is the only point at which it becomes real. Everything else is just fantasy.

—Jim Huling
Project Participant

· · ·

If you structure your daily review, you can take advantage of your mind's natural tendency to evaluate yourself and gain important insights that move you forward in your business and personal goals. Consider building into your routine a fifteen-minute reflective period at the end of your workday. In addition to holding yourself accountable in general, this is the opportunity to identify what you can learn from what happened and thereby improve your effectiveness in setting and achieving *smart* goals.

The following comments from Donald Treinen underscore the importance of having realistic criteria for how you evaluate the day. "I've learned in my almost fifty years of work life that no one and no solution is going to be perfect. So what we strive for is to get things about as close as we can and then to move on."

As you learn to manage the challenges of being a CEO and apply deliberate strategies to the management of your mind-body system, you should expect gradual improvements in your self-evaluations at the end of each day. Bringing both your personal and business life to their full potential through the synergy of your efforts is a noble and satisfying challenge.

ᵔᵔᵔᵔᵔᵔᵔᵔᵔᵔᵔᵔᵔᵔᵔᵔᵔᵔ

Make It Happen

Step One. Identify your leadership mind-set. How does this affect the way you manage workflow? Describe at least two positive attributes and two negative effects of your leadership approach. Can you gain by modifying the way you think about your role? If so, clarify the benefits you expect to gain by making this improvement. Build a plan for change.

Step Two. Consider how you manage disruptions. Identify three strategies that would help you to re-focus on your daily priorities and accomplish daily work goals. Choose one strategy that you will implement this week and make a specific plan for how you will do so.

Step Three. Consider your end of the day routine. How can you build in a structure for reviewing and evaluating your efforts? Create a template for monitoring your subjective and objective criteria for a day well spent. Implement your daily review for at least one week. At the end of that week, reflect on how effective it is, identify needed changes, and modify your template to improve it.

Sustaining Synergy for Success

Life is a creative, intimate, and unpredictable conversation
if it is nothing else, spoken or unspoken,
and our life and our work are both the result
of the particular way we hold that passionate conversation.

—David Whyte

It is my sincere hope this book will have a lasting impact on you in the most personal of ways: that you will go forward in your life believing that you really can have it all. I hope you will continue to vigorously pursue the career goals that mean so much to you, to work in ways that are invigorating and that bring out your best qualities, and to manage the interplay between your work life and your personal needs so that each improves the other. This is the essence of Synergy for Success. It is on this path of personal and professional growth that the highest and deepest levels of fulfillment are possible.

To sustain success in this way, you must be convinced that your efforts can produce the desired outcomes. When you are convinced that there are simple, but powerful, strategies that can help you to achieve your goals, then you are more likely to do the things that allow you to perform better, feel better, and be more satisfied in your work and in your personal life. That means you must do a sufficient number of the strategies recommended in this book enough times, *with deliberate practice*, so you get a clear sense of their benefits.

Try the strategies to see how they work. Actions are essential for behavioral change.

If you are not ready to engage in the process now, at least ask yourself, "What it will take for me to get ready?" Invariably, when I tell people about what is in this book, they proclaim, "Oh, wow. I sure need that!" Yet not everyone is ready to move on to the next phase, which involves *action*, not just *thought*. So as you arrive at the end of the book and proceed with the next phase of the process, where will you go? Do you need more convincing of the vital role of these methods in order for you to place them in the top tier of your priorities? If so, what will that take?

It is the strength of your *desire* that will compel you to take action. Early in the book, I urged you to develop your image of success—the good life, the life that is well worth living.

Does your desire include a high standard for your quality of life? Consider your day-to-day and hour-to-hour experience, the way you feel about yourself as a person at the end of the day, how satisfying your daily interactions are with friends and loved ones, how you feel when you bring the day to an end and when you begin the new day.

It is placing a high value on these aspects of life that will allow you to persist in doing what it takes. You have read the guidelines for managing the specific challenges, and I want to highlight here some important points to remember as you develop your strategies.

Synergy for Success

First and foremost, keep in mind that all the particulars, each specific strategy, is intended to be one of many components that, when blended together, become your *lifestyle*. To build the synergy that yields success in your life, you may have to take it on faith for a while that putting the ideas and strategies into action will foster an authentically fulfilling life.

Hardiness for Hard Times and Growth Mind-sets

The strategies in this book, in combination with a growth mind-set, will set you on the path to a hardy, fulfilling life. If you approach challenges as opportunities for personal and professional growth, and you seek to exercise commitment and control wherever possible, you will find ways to thrive. The information and guidelines in this book offer the best return on your investment. Use them as a starting point for developing what works best for you.

Become an Expert at Self-Improvement

Be sure to review and regularly use the guidelines for the process of change presented in chapter 3. In that way, you can assure yourself of using the best methods so your continued efforts feel worthwhile. Remember, your overriding goal should be embracing the *process* of making lifestyle changes. Be sure to pick one or two small changes at a time and master the process of sticking with them, rather than reaching for big and/or fast changes.

Frequently, people ask me about my lifestyle. They are particularly curious about my efforts in regard to eating, exercising, relaxation methods, meditation, and sleep hygiene. I reply that I live the life that I recommend, however I also point out that I have been building these habits, one step at a time, since I first had my medical crisis forty years ago.

Has it been a straight and consistent process? Absolutely not. Has it been easy and fun? Sometimes. Have the rewards been worth the effort? For sure! My wife and I derive great satisfaction when we reflect on how much better one of us is handling something today than at an earlier time in our lives (a private victory). The same is true when we are able to appreciate how much better we are now at handling relationship issues. These moments are some of the true joys of our lives.

Review, Refresh, Revise, Repeat

For many years, I wrote a monthly newsletter that addressed issues like the ones in this book. Invariably, I'd complete the newsletter and then find myself benefiting from it, as would my wife. We'd even joke about how this "well-known psychologist" advised doing such and such! It is not that it was new information for us. It was just the regular reminders that would enable us to realize again the value of some way of handling things better.

So, expect to need reminders from time to time. We are creatures of habit. Under pressure (distress), we revert to what we know the best. That is why it is important to practice these methods until they become routine. Return to the book for "booster" sessions, as needed. Reviewing portions of the book can revitalize your perspective. The more you come back to these smart ways of handling the pressures and challenges of your life, the more they will become integrated into your lifestyle.

Pausing

At the very beginning of the book, I presented the poem "Pausing." Take another look now and see what you make of it.

The poem captures the essence of the book: with all the stuff going on within you and all around you—the river in which *you* swim—you must be able to regularly pause, reflect upon what is happening, and generate the best strategy for proceeding, in order to reliably handle things well.

Return to the poem whenever you need a reminder of the value of a brief time out.

Personal Positioning System

When you frame each day as a journey, knowing where you are going and what you will need along the way helps your planning become more important. The personal positioning system (PPS) model offers a robust framework for you to *monitor* all of your resources and pressures. It allows you to consider your location in relation to your target destination(s), and thereby equips you to plan and adjust your route. Since your needs and circumstances will regularly change, be sure to review and revise it accordingly.

Daily Routines

Nobody, no matter how self-directed and self-sufficient, can just set his or her sails once and stay on the intended course. It is part of human nature to drift off course. So to sustain high levels of performance and a fulfilling life, you need routines and daily practices that serve as your guardrails.

You can turn each of the methods in this book into one. I recommend that you start with the morning ritual and the power break ritual. Both of these position your mind-set for dealing with the day. Then, gradually identify other routines that give you the biggest ROI.

Use deliberate practice so you can keep refining your methods and to offset the natural tendency for routines to become perfunctory. Keep in mind that each routine is a tool that should make your day go better. The greatest value comes from treating these as genuinely instrumental in making your day go better.

Professional and Personal Guardians

One of the most valuable things you can do, in addition to your own efforts to keep your-self functioning optimally, is to have a buddy system. Just imagine how comforting it would be to know that someone else is looking out for you—a guardian, a person who is invested in your success, well-being, and fulfillment; someone who can remind of your most important values and caution you when you have drifted too far off your best path.

As you increase your commitment to a life where you are functioning optimally at work and in your personal life, and you acquire a truly wise perspective on your human nature, you will see how helpful it is to have one or more guardians. Collaborate actively with each to set up the guidelines that work for you.

One True Friend

You need a true friend, someone with whom you can reveal your most personal feelings, and vent your wildest thoughts and urges. It must be someone who is mature enough to be comfortable with the raw stuff we all sometimes have within ourselves—from the natural emotional bile that builds up in the course of living a very engaged life to the lust, avarice, envy, and rage. When you have the freedom to vent those feelings and to have them appreciated by one who knows and loves you, it is tremendously relieving and comforting. It is especially nice when this special friend is also your life partner, but that is not a requirement.

Be Your Own Guardian

There is one final piece of advice that I have purposely saved for the end for fear of sounding too "touchy-feely." Here is how Pat Lynch, founder and CEO of Women's Online Media and Education Network, and editor-in-chief of WomensRadio and WomensCalendar, put it: "The most important thing is to love yourself. That's the hardest thing to do and it's the only thing to do. If you can do that early enough and then be of service to the world, wow, your joy begins."

As a CEO and high achiever, it is tempting to dismiss anything that is not clearly nuts and bolts and specific to the bottom line. Nevertheless, everything in this book *is* about loving yourself. By that I mean that you have to care about yourself, be considerate of yourself, and feel that you are worthy of being treated so well that you would put forth the effort it actually takes to create a full life.

Will You Make It Happen?

There is a tide in the affairs of men,
Which, taken at the flood, leads on to fortune,
Omitted, all the voyage of their life
Is bound in shallows and in miseries.
On such a full sea are we now afloat,
And we must take the current when it serves,
Or lose our ventures.

—Shakespeare, *Julius Caesar*

I encourage you to jump into the current and use the momentum to shift into action mode. Let each action step be your own vote of confidence, ensuring that you will keep your commitment to mastering the CEO's greatest challenge and building a fulfilling lifestyle.
Godspeed.

APPENDIX A

Making and Declining Requests

Six Key Components of an Effective Request

Be sure to note the basic distinction between a *request*, which gives the recipient the option of declining, and a *command*, based on your position of authority as a boss that does not give the option of declining.

1. Who, specifically, is making the request?

Take ownership for the request you are making. For example, say, "I would like to take some time off this afternoon to take my husband for his medical procedure." An unclear and nonspecific request is, "My husband wants me to be with him during his medical procedure this afternoon."

2. Who is the recipient of the request?

Identify clearly and specifically who it is that you are making the request of. Asking for "someone" to contact a client when several are present is not clear and specific.

3. What is the action that will fulfill your request?

Be as specific as possible about the action you are asking the person to take on your behalf. Asking a friend for support when you start a new job is vague and can easily lead to disappointment. She may think you want her to help you if you get emotionally discouraged. If you want her to provide backup childcare when the kids are sick, you could be unwittingly setting up a disappointment.

4. Is there sufficient common background to understand the request?

If there is any doubt that the recipient of your request may not know exactly what you are referring to, be sure to explain what you mean. Asking a new assistant to set up a business lunch with two people may require calling one person and e-mailing another. Not providing such guidelines is very likely to leave the assistant frustrated and unable to complete the request.

5. What is the specific time guideline that will satisfy the request?

Specify when you need what you are requesting. When asking your wife to review a letter you wrote, you need to specify when you need it by or she may do it at her convenience. If you need it by the next morning and have not conveyed this, she may say yes but fail to actually satisfy the request you had in mind.

6. Does your request provide the recipient with the opportunity to decline?

Make your request directly and explicitly so the recipient can know what is being agreed to or declined. The emphasis is on the behavioral act, not an implied judgment. Asking for something in an indirect manner contains a hidden judgment of the recipient's character. For example, "It sure would be nice if you would _____" implies that if the recipient does not comply, he or she is not nice.

Six Key Components of an Effective Decline

1. Be clear that it is the request for a specific action at a specific time that you are declining, not the relationship.

   "I am sorry, Jen, I wish I could help your preparations, but I've already promised Melissa I'd consult with her at that time."

2. Assist the requestor with making their request clearer, so you and they can be clear what it is you are declining.

   "I'm not sure if I can agree to do that or not. Please be more specific on what you are requesting. What are the guidelines for the report and when is the deadline?"

3. Say something explicitly, with a sincere and respectful tone that shows you are being sensitive to the impact of your decline to comply with their request.

   "Jen, I know the presentation you want me to review is crucial for your promotion, and that having my input would mean a lot to you. And I wish I could help."

4. Offer to assist in another way or at another time.

   "Even though I cannot be involved with editorial input for your presentation, I really want to support you in this. What are some other ways you could use help? Would you like me to listen to a practice run on it?"

5. Follow up at a later point to see how things turned out.

   "So, Jen, how did your presentation go? Would you like to meet sometime soon to review it?"

6. Provide a brief explanation for your need to decline that helps the other person have respect for your boundaries.

"Unfortunately, your time frame coincides with when I have to meet with the owners of a business to complete the final negotiations for a contract. Our alliance with this company is really important to us, and we've been working on the deal for the past three weeks."

REFERENCES

Allen, D. *Getting Things Done: The Art of Stress-Free Productivity.* New York: Penguin Books, 2003.

American Psychological Association. Special Issue on Happiness, Excellence, and Optimal Human Functioning. *American Psychologist,* 55(1), 1-200. 2000.

Ardelt, M. "Wisdom as Expert Knowledge System: A Critical Review of a Contemporary Operationalization of an Ancient Concept," *Human Development;*47:257-285. 2004.

Baltes, P. B., and U. M. Staudinger. "Wisdom: A Metaheuristic (Pragmatic) to Orchestrate Mind and Virtue toward Excellence," *American Psychologist,* 55, 122-135. 2000.

Barry, T. "Who's the Boss?" *Atlanta Business Chronicle,* August 12, 2002.

Bascomb, N. *The Perfect Mile: Three Athletes, One Goal, and Less than Four Minutes to Achieve It.* New York: Houghton Mifflin Harcourt, 2004.

Baumeister, R. F., K. D. Vohs, and D. M.Tice, "The Strength Model of Self-Control. *Current Directions in Psychological Science,* 16, 351-5. 2007.

Benson, H. *The Relaxation Response.* New York: HarperTorch, 2000.

Carmichael, C. *Food for Fitness.* New York: G. P. Putnam's and Sons, 2004.

Colvin, G. "What It Takes to be Great," *Fortune,* October 2006. http://money.cnn.com/magazines/fortune/fortune_archive/2006/10/30/toc.html.

Cooper-Kahn, J. and Laurie Dietzel. *Late, Lost, and Unprepared.* Bethesda, MD: Woodbine House, 2008.

Cooper-Kahn, J. and Margaret Foster. *Boosting Executive Skills in the Classroom: A Practical Guide for Teachers.* San Francisco, CA: Jossey-Bass, 2013.

Covey, S. *The 7 Habits of Highly Effective People.* New York: Free Press. 2004.

Covey, S., A. Roger Merrill, and Rebecca R. Merrill. *First Things First.* New York: Fireside, 1995.

Dweck, C. *Mindset: The New Psychology of Success.* New York: Ballantine Books, 2006.

Drucker, P. "Managing Oneself." *Harvard Business Review,* 62-74, 1999.

Elliot, A., and Carol S Dweck, Eds. *Handbook of Competence and Motivation*. New York: Guildford Press, 2005.

Ericsson, K. A., R.T. Krampe and C. Tesch-Römer "The Role of Deliberate Practice in the Acquisition of Expert Performance." *Psychological Review*, 100(3), 363-406, 1993.

Ericsson, K. A., and A.C. Lehmann "Expert and Exceptional Performance: Evidence on Maximal Adaptations on Task Constraints." *Annual Review of Psychology*, 47, 273-305. 1996.

Ericsson, K. A., C. Neil, R. R Hoffman,.and P. J. Feltovich, P. J., Eds. *The Cambridge Handbook of Expertise and Expert Performance*. New York: Cambridge University Press, 2006.

Fromm, E. *Escape from Freedom*. New York: Avon Books, 1941.

Gafni, M. *Soul Prints: Your Path to Fulfillment*. New York: Fireside, 2002.

Gallwey, W. Timothy. *The Inner Game of Tennis.*, New York: Bantam Books, 1974.

_____. *The Inner Game of Work*. New York: Random House, 2001.

Gates, B. "How I Work: Bill Gates," *Fortune*, April 2006.

Gioia, G. A., Peter K. Isquith, Steven C. Guy, and Lauren Kenworthy. *Behavior Rating Inventory of Executive Function, Professional Manual*. Odessa, FL: Psychological Assessment Resources, 2000.

Colvin, G. *Talent Is Overrated: What Really Separates World-Class Performers from Everybody Else*. New York: Penguin Group, 2010.

Gonzales, L. *Deep Survival: Who lives, Who dies, and Why*. New York: Norton, 2003.

Hill, N. *Think and Grow Rich*. New York: Ballantine Books, 1996.

Hopkins, M. S. "Why Leadership Is the Most Dangerous Idea in American Business," *Inc.*, 2007.

Howe, M. J. A., J. W. Davidson, and J. A. Sloboda. "Innate Gifts and Talents: Reality or Myth?" *Behavioral & Brain Sciences, 21*, 399-407, 1998.

Jiang, Y., R. Saxe, and N. Kanwisher. "Functional Magnetic Resonance Imaging Provides New Constraints on Theories of the Psychological Refractory Period," *Psychological Science*, 15 (6) 390-6, 2004.

Kahn, M. H. "Stress Management for Entrepreneurs," *Entrepreneurs Exchange Resource Guide*, 16, 1990.

_____. "Managing the Stress of Ambition," *Annapolis and Anne Arundel County Chamber News*, 2(7), 5-7, 2000.

_____. "Vacation Wisdom To Help You Set, Achieve Goals," *SELL!NG*, 7, 12, 2001.

_____. "Build Stamina for Stress with Hardiness Training,". *SELL!NG*, 11, 13, 2001.

_____. "Hardiness Training." www.advisortoday.com/archives/2002_may_kahn.html.

_____. "Create Your Own Performance Rituals and Perform like a Sales Champion," *SELL!NG*, 6, 10-11, 2002.

Kaplan, S. and Marc G. Berman. "Directed Attention as a Common Resource for Executive Functioning and Self-Regulation," *Perspectives on Psychological Science*, 5(1) 43-57, 2010.

Keen, S. *Fire in the Belly: On Being a Man*. New York: Bantam, 1992.

Kehaulani Goo, S. "Building a 'Googley' Workforce: Corporate Culture Breeds Innovation," *Washington Post*, 2006.

Kilburg, R. R. *Executive Wisdom: Coaching and the Emergence of Virtuous Leaders*. Washington, DC: American Psychological Association, 2006.

Kobasa, S. C. "Personality and Resistance to Illness," *American Journal of Community Psychology*, 7, 413-23. 1979.

_____. "Stressful Life Events, Personality, and Health: An Inquiry into Hardiness," *Journal of Personality and Social Psychology*, 37, 1-11. 1979.

Kurson, R. *Shadow Divers: The True Adventure of Two Americans Who Risked Everything to Solve One of the Last Mysteries of World War II*, New York: Random House, 2004.

Lakhani, D. *Power of an Hour: Business and Life Mastery in One Hour A Week*, New Jersey: Wiley, 2006.

Leonard, G. *Mastery: The Keys to Success and Long-Term Fulfillment*. New York: Plume, 1992.

Loehr, J. *Toughness Training for Life*, New York: Penguin Books, 1994.

_____. *Stress for Success*, New York: Three Rivers Press, 1997.

Loehr, J. and Tony Schwartz. *The Power of Full Engagement: Managing Energy, Not Time, Is the Key to High Performance and Personal Renewal*. New York: Free Press, 2003.

Maddi, S. R. and S. C. Kobasa. *The Hardy Executive: Health under Stress*, Homewood, Ill: Dow Jones-Irwin, 1984.

_____. *Resilience at Work: How to Succeed no Matter What Life Throws at You*. New York: AMACOM Books, 2005.

Norcross, J., James Procheska, and Carlo DiClemente. *Changing For Good.* New York: Harper-Collins, 1994.

Orman, M. *The 14-Day Stress Cure.* Houston, Texas: Breakthru Publishing, 1991.

Quinlan, M. L. *Time off for Good Behavior: How Hardworking Women Can Take a Break and Change Their Lives,* New York: Broadway Books, 2005.

Polivy, J. and C. P. Herman. "If at First You Don't Succeed: False Hopes of Self-Change," *American Psychologist,* 57, 677-89, 2002.

Reps, P. *Juicing.* Garden City, New York: Anchor Books, 1978.

Roizen, M. F., and Mehmet C. Oz. *You: The Owner's Manual,* New York: Collins, 2008.

Rossi, E. L. *The Twenty-Minute Break,* Los Angeles, CA: J. P. Tarcher, 1991.

Rubinstein, J. S., D. E. Meyer, and J. E. Evans. "Executive Control of Cognitive Processes in Task Switching," *Journal of Experimental Psychology: Human Perception and Performance,* 27, 763-97, 2001.

Sapolsky, R. M. *Why Zebras Don't Get Ulcers.* New York: Holt Publishing, 2004.

_____. Sympathy for the CEO. *Science.* 333(6040):293-4. 2011.

_____. "The Importance of a Sense of Control and the Physiological Benefits of Leadership," Prepublication communication, 2012.

Schmeichel, B. J., K. D.Vohs, and R. F. Baumeister, "Intellectual Performance and Ego Depletion: Role of the Self in Logical Reasoning and Other Information Processing," *Journal of Personality and Social Psychology.* Vol. 85, No. 1, 33-46, 2003.

Schwartz, T., and C. McCarthy. "Manage Your Energy, Not Your Time,". *Harvard Business Review,* reprint R0710B, 2007.

Seligman, M. E. P. *Authentic Happiness: Using the New Positive Psychology to Realize Your Potential for Deep Fulfillment.* Boston, MA: Nicholas Brealey Publishing, 2002.

Sendak, M. *Where the Wild Things Are.* New York: Harper Collins, 2012.

Sherman, G. D., J. J. Lee, A. J. C. Cuddy, et al. "Leadership Is Associated with Lower Levels of Stress," *Proceedings of the National Academy of Sciences.* http://www.pnas.org/content/early/2012/09/19/1207042109.

Siebert, A. *The Resiliency Advantage: Master Change, Thrive under Pressure, and Bounce Back from Setbacks.* San Francisco, CA: Berrett-Koehler Publishers, 2005.

Siebert, K. W. and M. W. Daudelin. *The Role of Reflection in Managerial Learning.* Westport, CT: Quorum, 1999.

Spencer, J. "Are You Stressed out Yet?—No Wonder: Research Shows People Handle Anxiety Wrong; the Case against the Spa," The *Wall Street Journal,* 2003.

Stengel, R. "Mandela: His Eight Lessons of Leadership," *Time* magazine, 2008.

Watts, A. *The Book: on the Taboo against Knowing Who You Are.* New York: Random House, 1972.

Wever, R. *The Circadian System of Man.* New York: Springer-Verlag, 1979.

Whyte, D. *The Heart Aroused: Poetry and the Preservation of the Soul in Corporate America.* New York: Doubleday. 1994

_____. *Crossing the Unknown Sea: Work as a Pilgrimage of Identity.* New York: Riverhead. 2001

_____. *The Three Marriages: Reimagining Work, Self, and Relationship,* New York: Riverhead. 2009.

Yeager, C. *Yeager: An Autobiography,* New York: Bantam. 1986.

Zilbergeld, B. and Arnold A. Lazararus. *Mind Power: Getting What You Want through Mental Training,* Boston: Little, Brown, and Company, 1987.

NOTES

Preface

1. Kobasa 1979a and b.
2. Kobassa 1979a and b; Maddi and Kobassa, 1984.
3. http://www.mhkcoaching.com/index.php/ceostressproject.
4. http://www.mhkcoaching.com/index.php/stressmgt.

Introduction

5. A partial listing of participants (some felt it necessary to remain anonymous) can be viewed at http://www.mhkcoaching.com/index.php/ceostressproject.
6. Throughout the book I use the Chief Executive Officer (CEO) as the prototype for those roles where similar pressures and challenges exist, including rising business executives and entrepreneurs.
7. Throughout the book I use self-management as the general term for managing oneself. One aspect of self-management is self-care, which I use to refer to basic matters such as rest, sleep, nutrition, and exercise.
8. Ming-Jer Chen, *Washington Post*, July 8, 2012, p. G-2.
9. Kobasa 1979a and b.
10. Maddi and Kobasa 1984; Maddi and Khoshaba 2005.
11. Sherman, G., Lee, J., Cuddy, A. et al. 2012. See also Sapolsky's 2012 comments on this research.
12. Note that the terms mind-body and brain-body are being used synonymously throughout the book.
13. Dweck 2006.
14. Watts 1972.

Chapter 1 The Challenges of CEOs

15. Watts 1972.
16. James Loehr (1994) is the originator of the concept of the ideal performance state. I have adapted that concept to apply specifically to the performance of an executive.
17. Kahn 1990.
18. Whyte 2009, 26.

[19]   Whyte 1994 and 2001.

[20]   Kilburg 2006.

[21]   Ibid.

[22]   Cooper-Kahn and Foster 2013.

[23]   This important dynamic is explained in detail in chapter 4.

[24]   Covey 2004.

[25]   Sendak 2012.

[26]   Covey 2004.

[27]   Gallwey 2001.

[28]   Kilburg 2006.

[29]   Loehr 1994 and 1997, and Loehr and Schwartz 2003.

Chapter 2 The Successful Executive

[30]   Maddi and Kobasa 1984, Maddi and Khoshaba 2005.

[31]   Rossi 1991.

[32]   Siebert 2005.

[33]   Hill 1996.

[34]   Covey 1995.

[35]   Loehr 1994 and 1997.

[36]   Seeligman 2002.

[37]   Gafni 2002.

[38]   American Psychological Association 2002.

[39]   See the inspiring reflection on this at http://www.businesstheatre.com/Graphics/Death%20Is%20Not%20The%20Enemy.pdf.

[40]   I urge you to read the poem "The Invitation" by Oriah Mountain Dreamer. It is available on the Internet.

[41]   You can download the form at www.mhkcoaching.com/masteryforms

Chapter 3 The Myth of Natural Talent

[42]   http://en.wikiquote.org/wiki/Bee_Movie.

[43]   Zilbergeld, B. and Arnold Lazararus (1987). The true story of this event is wonderfully captured in *The Perfect Mile* by Neal Bascomb (2004).

[44]   This research is nicely summarized in the article "What it takes to be great" by Geoffrey Colvin. The original studies are in Ericsson et al. 1993, 1996, and 2006, and Howe et al. 1998.

[45]   Ibid.

46 http://faculty.washington.edu/chudler/plast.html.

47 See Polivy and Herman 2002 for a detailed explanation of what they call the "false-hope syndrome" which they characterize as a "cycle of failure and renewed effort ... characterized by unrealistic expectations about the likely speed, amount, ease, and consequences of self-change attempts."

48 For a deeper understanding of the process of change together with more detailed guidelines, I highly recommend the following books, *Changing for Good,* by Norcross, Procheska, and DiClemente; and *Mastery* by Leonard.

49 Kilburg 2006.

50 Norcross, Procheska, and DiClemente 1994.

51 Covey 2004.

52 Ibid.

53 Ibid.

54 This is the method Gary Jobs, one of the all-time greatest sailors, used to develop his skills.

55 Sapolsky 2004.

56 Rossi 1991.

57 Sapolsky 2004.

58 Kaplan and Berman 2010, 45.

59 Kaplan and Berman 2010, 46.

60 Schmeichel, Vohs, and Baumeister 2003.

61 Ibid.

62 Baumeister, Vohs, and Tice, 2007.

63 Spencer 2003.

64 Loehr and Schwartz 2003.

65 To bolster your resolve, read about the path to mastery described by Leonard (1992).

66 Stephen Covey has nicely framed this as managing your life by using a compass.

67 See additional guidelines for the buddy system in chapter 12.

68 Whyte 2009.

69 Whyte 2009, 11.

70 In my not-so-humble opinion, these are the most effective strategies you can use to maintain your inner equilibrium and thereby to stay cool and function well!

71 Kaplan and Berman 2010. Their review of research on attention restoration therapy (ART) explains the value of meditation and walking as effective means of allowing our efforts at directed attention to recover. During ART our minds can enter into a "soft fascination" (48) with matters. In so doing, we can become aware of other useful thoughts and concerns.

[72] For an in-depth understanding of the psychology of freedom, read the classic treatise on the matter, *Escape from Freedom* by Erich Fromm 1941.

[73] This is a main factor in any compulsive activity, such as eating or smoking. The underlying objective of the behavior is to calm oneself, not to gain weight or cause cancer. It is sad, but true, that in many work settings, people are permitted to take a smoking break, but not a break to calm or refresh themselves!

[74] Benson 2000.

Chapter 5 Regulating Your Operating System

[75] Steps 4-9 have been adapted, with permission, from a six-step stress reduction method published by Mort Orman, MD, in *The 14 Day Stress Cure*, 1991.

[76] Seligman 2002.

[77] Drucker 1999.

[78] It is noteworthy that whereas most professional licenses require ongoing continuing education to maintain competency, generally no such requirements exist for business executives.

[79] This is a nice example of what you should be looking for when you use the nine-step stress management method described in chapter 5.

[80] Chris Carmichael (2004) is an expert on how to use food as fuel for good energy. Another good source of general healthy eating guidelines is the writings of Michael Roizen and Mehmet C. Oz (2008).

[81] Carmichael 2004.

[82] Loehr and Schwartz 2003.

[83] The present guidelines assume that a thorough medical examination has already taken place to rule out underlying medical conditions that may be causing difficulty with sleep.

[84] http://stopthesilence.org/.

[85] Loehr 1994 and 1997, and Loehr and Schwartz 2003.

[86] Rossi 1991.

[87] http://www.apa.org/news/press/releases/2001/08/multitasking.aspx; http://www.forbes.com/sites/carolkinseygoman/2011/04/26/the-myth-of-multitasking/

[88] There are numerous scientific studies of multitasking showing very real limitations in functional ability that can happen. See, for example, Rubinstein, Meyer, and Evans 2001; Jiang, Saxe, and Kanwisher 2004.

See also Research at Stanford's Memory Laboratory and Carnegie Mellon's Center for Cognitive Brain Imagery. http://news.stanford.edu/news/2009/

august24/multitask-research-study-082409.html

[89] Lakhani 2006.

[90] Keene 1992.

Chapter 9 Renewing Yourself

[91] Fromm 1941.

[92] Whyte 1994, p. 266 uses the poem "Love after Love" by Derek Walcott to convey this. It is available on the Internet.

[93] Kaplan and Berman 2010.

Chapter 10 Executive Cool

[94] Gonzales 2004.

[95] Kilburg 2006.

[96] Seibert and Daudelin 1999.

[97] Stengel 2008.

Chapter 11 Recovering Your Cool

[98] Yeager 1986.

[99] Keen 1992.

[100] Hill 1996.

[101] See guidelines for setting up a buddy system in chapter 12.

Chapter 12 Managing Relationships

[102] Kehaulani Goo 2006.

[103] See chapter 3.

[104] There are many dimensions to what are sometimes referred to as shadow negotiations. See Fisher and Patton 2011; Kolb and Williams 2003.

[105] Quinlan 2005.

[106] Two excellent guidelines on the practical methods for managing workflow are *First Things First* by Stephen Covey and *Getting Things Done: The Art of Stress-Free Productivity* by David Allen. You will find the methods in those books immensely helpful. Use them.

Chapter 13 Managing Workflow

[107] Hopkins 2007.

[108] David Allen (2003) has written extensively on ways to organize oneself to improve productivity. If you need more detailed information about how to organize for maximum productivity, his guidelines are definitely worth reading.

[109] Gates 2006.

INDEX

Page numbers followed by *n* indicate note numbers.

the battle within, 3-5
to drift off intended course, 206
to evaluate performance at the
end of the day, 200-201
to maintain equilibrium, 36
to simplify complex matters, 63
value of pausing to get
perspective, 63-65
Hypnosis, 20–22
self, 64–65

I

Ideal executive performance state
defined, 3
executive cool, 123-124
managing disruptions, 196
managing mind-body operating
system, 49-50
self-maintenance for
foundation, 83-96
valued by successful CEOs, 46
Ideal performance state (IPS), 16
Illinois Bell Study, xviii
Inbox, managing, 198–200
Information overload and
underload, 200
Insomnia, 92

J

Jules Feiffer, 49-50
Just Noticeable Difference (JND)
described, 42–43
evidence of improvement, 71,
82, 100

K

Kaplan, Stephen, 55
Kekich, David, 184
Kelley, Ed, 106, 150, 189
Khoshaba, D. M., vi, 49
Kilburg, Richard R., 12, 184
Kobasa, Suzanne, xviii–xix
Kurson, Robert, 132

L

Langrall, Clarke, Jr., 196
Leadership
antiheroic model, 186
becoming a wise leader, 5–7
dealing with office tensions,
171–172
mind-set for managing
workflow, 185–188
Leis, Alan, 12, 171–172, 179
Letting go of the day, 108-109
Lifestyle
life as journey, 18–20
life events, 19
making routines a natural part
of lifestyle, 204, 206
nonwork aspects of life, 8,
116–122
reflecting on a life worth living,
20–21
self-renewal, 116–122
the good life, 17–26
work-life balance, 17
Loehr, James, 12, 16, 83, 94, 95, 98,
219n16

to regain good energy after
using power break ritual,
107-108

V

Verrecchia, Al, 120

W

Wakeup call, xvii, 9
Watts, Alan, 2
Well-being
benefit of pausing, 63-65
choosing to disengage from
pressures to bolster, 121
derived from having a guardian,
206-207
described, 39
energy derived from good
fit with role and work
environment, 25, 85, 125
energy derived from personal
and social well-being, 88
importance of supportive
relationships, 7
personal success equation, 12
satisfaction with having a good
day at work, 98
source of strength, 85–88, 125
"White-collar athletes," 57, 88, 89.
Whyte, David, 3, 4, 62, 203
Wilcox, Ella Wheeler, 14
Will
key component of mind-set for
change, 36
Wingrove, Clinton, 1, 86, 99–100,
148, 192

Winter, Captain Jeffrey, 141, 164
Wisdom, xxv, 7, 11, 19, 20, 26, 36,
45, 83, 145, 157, 188, 196
Workday. *See also* Workplace,
Working smarter, Workflow,
Staff
art of the fresh start, 105–106
benefits of strategic use of
breaks, 69
engaging the day the hardiness
way, 98-103
guidelines for working smarter,
113-115
Hardiness for Hard Times
ritual, 101–102
importance of "user-friendly"
schedule with wiggle
room, 192-193
improving self-monitoring, 104
letting go of the day, 108–109
key aspects of company culture
that reduce distress at the
top, 161-165
key performance objectives, 185
managing energy to foster
optimal performance,
83-96
managing interpersonal
pressures to reduce
distress, 172
managing nutrition to fuel
performance, 88-90
managing workflow, 184–202
morning ritual, 102–103
satisfaction with personal
performance, 24-25, 98,
200-201
staying energized, 103–108

Made in the USA
Middletown, DE
13 March 2020